Designing the *Life of Johnson*

DESIGNING THE
Life of Johnson

THE LYELL LECTURES, 2001–2

Bruce Redford

OXFORD
UNIVERSITY PRESS

OXFORD
UNIVERSITY PRESS

Great Clarendon Street, Oxford OX2 6DP

Oxford University Press is a department of the University of Oxford.
It furthers the University's objective of excellence in research, scholarship,
and education by publishing worldwide in

Oxford New York

Auckland Cape Town Dar es Salaam Hong Kong Karachi
Kuala Lumpur Madrid Melbourne Mexico City Nairobi
New Delhi Shanghai Taipei Toronto

With offices in

Argentina Austria Brazil Chile Czech Republic France Greece
Guatemala Hungary Italy Japan Poland Portugal Singapore
South Korea Switzerland Thailand Turkey Ukraine Vietnam

Oxford is a registered trade mark of Oxford University Press
in the UK and in certain other countries

Published in the United States
by Oxford University Press Inc., New York

British Library Cataloguing in Publication Data
Data available

Library of Congress Cataloging in Publication Data
Redford, Bruce.
Designing the life of Johnson / Bruce Redford.
(The Lyell lectures; 2001–2)
Includes bibliographical references and index.
1. Boswell, James, 1740–1795. Life of Samuel Johnson. 2. Authors,
English—Biography—History and criticism. 3. Johnson, Samuel, 1709–1784.
4. Biography as a literary form. I. Title. II. Series.
PR3533.B7 R44 2002   828'.609–dc21   2001058824

Typeset by Regent Typesetting, London
Printed in Great Britain
on acid-free paper by
Biddles Ltd, King's Lynn, Norfolk

ISBN 0–19–818739–4 978–0–19–818739–4
ISBN 0–19–928483–0 (Pbk.) 978–0–19–928483–2 (Pbk.)

1 3 5 7 9 10 8 6 4 2

For Stuart Sherman
and in memory of
D. F. McKenzie

ACKNOWLEDGEMENTS

The Electors to the J. P. R. Lyell Readership in Bibliography did me the honour of issuing the invitation, Oxford University Press that of making the transient, permanent. The Press's readers and editors set the highest standards of professional expertise.

For stimulus and support I am deeply grateful to Mary, Viscountess Eccles, Professor Stephen Fix, Professor Rachel Jacoff, Professor Roger Lonsdale, the Revd Dr Michael F. Suarez, SJ, and Dr Richard Wendorf. Professor Allen Reddick, Professor Susan Staves, and Professor Howard D. Weinbrot provided stimulating forums for the discussion of the *Life* manuscript. This project is rooted in a twenty-year association with the Yale Boswell Editions, whose staff both past and present I thank for their support.

In Chapter 3 I draw upon 'Talk into Text: The Shaping of Conversation in Boswell's *Life of Johnson*', in Howard D. Weinbrot, Peter J. Schakel, and Stephen E. Karian (eds.), *Eighteenth-Century Contexts: Historical Inquiries in Honor of Phillip Harth*, (Madison: University of Wisconsin Press, 2001), 247–64. Chapter 5 makes use of 'Taming Savage Johnson', *Literary Imagination*, 1 (1999), 85–101. I am grateful to the University of Wisconsin Press and to the editor of *Literary Imagination* for permission to incorporate portions of these essays into the Lyell Lectures.

CONTENTS

LIST OF ILLUSTRATIONS

(between pages 80 and 81)

1, 2. MS leaves 1037ᵛ and 1038ʳ: in keeping with the compositional method he had adopted at the outset, Boswell has drafted his narrative on the recto and used the facing verso for additions and/or revisions (Beinecke Rare Book and Manuscript Library, Yale University).

3. MS leaf 545ʳ: the signature mark (designating Sheet G of volume ii) appears in the lower left-hand margin (by permission of the Houghton Library, Harvard University, fMS Eng 1836).

4. The cancellandum that reveals Johnson's authorship of dedications for both Reynolds and Percy; Boswell has supplied the text for the cancellans at the top of the page (Beinecke Rare Book and Manuscript Library, Yale University).

5. The earliest version of the title-page, corrected by Boswell and annotated by Thomas Edlyne Tomlins: 'The above was the first Matter pulled in Mr. Baldwin's New Printing Office, Union street Bridge Street Blackfriars. Monday 9 Mar. 1789' (Beinecke Rare Book and Manuscript Library, Yale University).

CUE TITLES

Baker

The Correspondence of James Boswell with David Garrick, Edmund Burke, and Edmond Malone, ed. Peter S. Baker et al. (London: Heinemann, 1986).

Brady

Frank Brady, *James Boswell: The Later Years 1769–1795* (New York: McGraw-Hill, 1984).

Great Biographer

Boswell: The Great Biographer 1789–1795, ed. Marlies K. Danziger and Frank Brady (New York: McGraw-Hill, 1989).

Letters

The Letters of Samuel Johnson, ed. Bruce Redford, 5 vols. (Princeton: Princeton Univ. Press, 1992–4).

Life

Boswell's Life of Johnson, ed. G. B. Hill, rev. L. F. Powell, 6 vols. (Oxford: Clarendon Press, 1934–50; vols. v–vi, rev. 1964).

Life MS i, ii

James Boswell's Life of Johnson: An Edition of the Original Manuscript in Four Volumes (Edinburgh Univ. Press and Yale Univ. Press, 1994–). Vol. i: *1709–1765*, ed. Marshall Waingrow; Volume ii: *1766–1776*, ed. Bruce Redford, with Elizabeth Goldring.

Literary Career   Frederick A. Pottle, *The Literary Career of James Boswell, Esq.* (Oxford: Clarendon Press, 1929).

Waingrow   *The Correspondence and Other Papers of James Boswell Relating to the Making of the* Life of Johnson, ed. Marshall Waingrow, 2nd edn. (Edinburgh: Edinburgh Univ. Press and Yale Univ. Press, 2001).

TEXTUAL NOTE

The Yale edition of the manuscript of Boswell's *Life* has been planned in four volumes, which are keyed to the standard Hill–Powell edition. Two volumes have been published thus far; these two, which cover the period 1709–76, present a transcription of MS leaves 1–550. The unpublished portion of the manuscript is divided between the Houghton Library, Harvard University, and the Beinecke Library, Yale University. Quotations from this material are referenced by leaf number; unless otherwise noted, the leaf belongs to the Beinecke's portion of the MS. In every instance the transcription follows the method devised by Marshall Waingrow and described in the introduction to volume i of the Yale edition.

Introduction

It seems both ungracious and unwise to begin by disagreeing with Virginia Woolf, whose reflections on finishing her life of Roger Fry reveal a keen understanding of the biographical enterprise. 'What a curious relation is mine with Roger at this moment,' Woolf notes in her diary, 'I who have given him a kind of shape after his death—Was he like that? I feel very much in his presence at the moment: as if I were intimately connected with him.'[1] Shape, presence, connection: in meditating upon these three Woolf makes an implicit case for the imaginative power of a form she both prized and practised. Yet in her public writings she allows herself to argue that biography offers both 'a different life from the life of poetry and fiction' and 'a life lived at a lower degree of tension'.[2] Woolf claims further that the biographer is 'a craftsman, not an artist; and his work is not a work of art but something betwixt and between'.[3] This dismissive judgement not only slights the mystery inherent in the word itself—'biography', the writing (*graphein*) of a life (*bios*)—it also denies the biographer an artist's prerogative. Even now, when biography is ardently practised and avidly consumed, we are still grappling with a version of Woolf's question: is the biographer a craftsman or an artist? It is still possible, to take one recent example, for a John Barrell to find fault with a Richard Holmes for giving way to 'the artist's desire to reshape his

[1] *The Diary of Virginia Woolf*, v: *1936–1941*, ed. Anne Olivier Bell (New York: Harcourt Brace Jovanovich, 1984), 305 (entry for 25 July 1940).

[2] Woolf, 'The Art of Biography', in *The Death of the Moth and Other Essays* (New York: Harcourt, Brace and Co., 1942), 195.

[3] Ibid. 196.

material'.[4] Holmes himself wittily reworks Woolf's 'betwixt and between' when he speaks of biography as 'a brilliant, bastard form'—the result of 'an Unholy Alliance' in which 'Fiction married Fact, without benefit of clergy'.[5] What to make *of* and do *with* their illegitimate offspring?

Such questions have no easy answers, witness the conflicting criteria for biographical excellence or even the lack of any criteria at all. One reason for this perplexed state of affairs is the fact that we are still operating under the influence of Aristotle's categorical distinction between 'history' and 'poetry'. In chapter 9 of his *Poetics*, Aristotle maintains that 'poetry is more philosophical and more elevated than history, since poetry relates more of the universal, while history relates particulars.'[6] Aristotle further implies that the real and the imaginary present antagonistic claims. Ever since the genre began to flourish in the eighteenth century, readers and practitioners alike have tended to place biography firmly in the historical camp by insisting that its factual status takes absolute precedence over any possible claim to poetic autonomy. Another way of expressing this view is to say that correspondence has trumped coherence in assessing the biographical artefact. My own conviction—a conviction these lectures aspire to impart—is that biography can and should mediate between history and poetry, the particular and the universal. Informing my analysis is the premiss that a successful biography both *reflects* a contingent reality (which can be verified outside the text) and *creates* an internal reality of its own (whose hallmark is what the eighteenth

---

[4] Hermione Lee quoting John Barrell in Lee, 'Tracking the Untrackable', *New York Review of Books*, 48/6 (12 Apr. 2001), 53.

[5] Holmes, 'Biography: Inventing the Truth', in John Batchelor (ed.), *The Art of Literary Biography* (Oxford: Clarendon Press, 1995), 15.

[6] Aristotle, *Poetics*, ed. and trans. Stephen Halliwell (Cambridge, Mass.: Harvard Univ. Press, 1995), 59 (Loeb Classical Library).

century would have called 'integrity'). To write a life is to design a life.

Yet designing is not the same as fabricating. As Samuel Johnson emphasizes in his *Rambler* essay on biography, 'no species of writing . . . can more certainly enchain the heart by irresistible interest'; it can only do so, however, by creating what Johnson calls 'a judicious and faithful narrative'.[7] The biographer's faithfulness consists above all in a tireless search for the most complete and the most reliable evidence. Like Boswell, he must spare 'no pains to ascertain [innumerable detached particulars] with a scrupulous authenticity', 'to run half over London, in order to fix a date correctly'.[8] A 'judicious' narrative depends in part upon the biographer's ability, once the evidence has been collected, to evaluate the 'innumerable detached particulars' according to rigorous criteria of authenticity. The same skills also affect the choice and the positioning of evidence. Economy joined to maximum power of evocation—a pairing that Leon Edel has called 'high selection'—is the hallmark of all judicious biography.[9] One might speak as well of 'high fidelity', which derives from a paradoxical combination of objective assessment and emotional commitment. Adulation, hostility, and indifference—in their different but comparably damaging ways, these sabotage the undertaking. Only a few biographers have been able first to strike and then to sustain a posture of intensely controlled subjectivity.

Boswell is one of them. In writing about him as autobiographer, W. K. Wimsatt rings the changes on a single, resonant phrase, 'the fact imagined'.[10] Wimsatt's phrase applies to

---

[7] Johnson, *The Rambler*, ed. W. J. Bate and Albrecht B. Strauss, 3 vols. (New Haven: Yale Univ. Press, 1969), i. 319–20 (No. 60).   [8] *Life* i. 7.

[9] Edel, *Writing Lives: Principia Biographica* (New York: W. W. Norton, 1984), 35.

[10] Wimsatt, 'The Fact Imagined: James Boswell', in *Hateful Contraries: Studies in Literature and Criticism* (Lexington: Univ. of Kentucky Press, 1965), 165–83.

biography as well, distilling into a seeming paradox its responsibility to the twin claims of fact and art. This responsibility brings with it both exhilarating resources and commanding restraints. Indeed the restraints are themselves resources, as Boswell's *magnum opus* helps us to understand. Over and over again the *Life of Johnson* demonstrates how the biographer's service can be perfect freedom—nowhere more incisively than in a haunting conversation about the fear of death, in which Boswell weaves together a record of the actual exchange with a powerful comparison. We will be considering this passage in some detail at a later stage of our investigation. At the moment I want to offer Boswell's daring move as an example of history and poetry in perfect counterpoint:

His mind resembled the vast amphitheatre, the Colisaeum at Rome. In the centre stood his judgement, which, like a mighty gladiator, combated those apprehensions that, like the wild beasts of the *Arena*, were all around in cells, ready to be let out upon him. After a conflict, he drove them back into their dens; but not killing them, they were still assailing him.[11]

The biographer-poet enters the mind of his epic hero and illuminates it with an epic simile: not a metaphor, which might conflate the historical and the poetic, but a simile, which differentiates as it aligns. Boswell records, interprets, and intensifies—fulfilling in his own fashion Johnson's desire that a biographer place us, 'for a time, in the condition of him whose fortune we contemplate'.[12]

At such moments Boswell both tests and respects the boundaries of biography. To draw those boundaries with greater precision, let's consider briefly two works that confront the ultimate narrative problem, how to render the experience of dying. The

---

[11] *Life* ii. 106 (26 Oct. 1769).
[12] *Rambler* No. 60, ed. Bate and Strauss, i. 319.

first of these, Katherine Anne Porter's 'The Jilting of Granny Weatherall', is a short story; the second, Lytton Strachey's *Queen Victoria*, is a biography that aspires to revivify 'the most delicate and humane of all the branches of the art of writing'.[13] Both Porter and Strachey make use of stream-of-consciousness narrative to capture the protagonist's final moments.

As she lies dying, Porter's Granny Weatherall ranges back over the events of her long life. Through synecdochic fragments Porter recreates the experience of a woman who has been cruelly abandoned at the altar and is about to be cruelly abandoned again. The story ends with the ultimate act of jilting:

> The blue light from Cornelia's lampshade drew into a tiny point in the center of her brain, it flickered and winked like an eye, quietly it fluttered and dwindled. Granny lay curled down within herself, amazed and watchful, staring at the point of light that was herself; her body was now only a deeper mass of shadow in an endless darkness and this darkness would curl around the light and swallow it up. God, give a sign!
>
> For the second time there was no sign. Again no bridegroom and the priest in the house. She could not remember any other sorrow because this grief wiped them all away. Oh, no, there's nothing more cruel than this—I'll never forgive it. She stretched herself with a deep breath and blew out the light.[14]

Porter's narrative achieves its devastating impact because we never stop to question the authenticity of the experience it describes. Even as we register the artifice (the echoes of the Gospel of John, the double meaning of 'bridegroom') we are drawn irresistibly into the flickering consciousness of Granny Weatherall. In fact, we are drawn in because of the artifice: 'the

---

[13] Preface to *Eminent Victorians* (New York: Harcourt Brace Jovanovich, n.d.), p. viii.

[14] Katherine Anne Porter, *Flowering Judas and Other Stories* (New York: Harcourt, Brace and World, 1958), 136.

truest poetry', as Touchstone tells Audrey, 'is the most feigning.' And this is poetry—pure invention, related to the domain of fact but not accountable to it.

As she lies dying, Strachey's Queen Victoria ranges back over the events of her long life. Strachey decides to bring his biography to a close and to unify our disparate impressions of Victoria by running the film of her life backwards, pausing momentarily at certain suggestive stages. In one long sentence, the Queen's mind wanders dreamily from old age to extreme youth. The result is a vivid montage:

She herself, as she lay blind and silent, seemed to those who watched her to be divested of all thinking—to have glided already, unawares, into oblivion. Yet, perhaps, in the secret chambers of consciousness, she had her thoughts, too. Perhaps her fading mind called up once more the shadows of the past to float before it, and retraced, for the last time, the vanished visions of that long history—passing back and back, through the cloud of years, to older and ever older memories—to the spring woods at Osborne, so full of primroses for Lord Beaconsfield— to Lord Palmerston's queer clothes and high demeanour, and Albert's face under the green lamp, and Albert's first stag at Balmoral, and Albert in his blue and silver uniform, and the Baron coming in through a doorway, and Lord M. dreaming at Windsor with the rooks cawing in the elm-trees, and the Archbishop of Canterbury on his knees in the dawn, and the old King's turkey-cock ejaculations, and Uncle Leopold's soft voice at Claremont, and Lehzen with the globes, and her mother's feathers sweeping down towards her, and a great old repeater-watch of her father's in its tortoise-shell case, and a yellow rug, and some friendly flounces of sprigged muslin, and the trees and the grass at Kensington.[15]

By forging a chain of significant people and evocative places, Strachey invites us to relive his biography at top speed: significant parts of a life imply and complete the whole. As a rhetorical tour

---

[15] Strachey, *Queen Victoria* (New York: Harcourt Brace and Co., 1921), 423–4.

de force and a means of achieving structural unity, the passage compels a certain kind of admiration: it would be difficult to deny that Strachey has found a way of fulfilling his call for biographical writing that is 'delicate and humane'. At the same time, however, Strachey's conclusion 'feigns' in a way that betrays rather than fulfils the biographer's calling. First, the flashback sacrifices history to poetry: a reliable eyewitness testifies that Victoria was not silent on her deathbed; furthermore, her last coherent word, 'Bertie', suggests that she was brooding at the last over the errant Prince of Wales.[16] Strachey quietly, even disingenuously, attempts to cover himself by inserting the word 'perhaps'—yet the entire passage dedicates itself to quashing whatever disbelief that word might arouse. Second, the rhetorical contrivance backfires: instead of bringing our acquaintance with Victoria to a climax, it distances us by making the versatile biographer the true protagonist of his tale. Unlike the figurative language and the echoing repetitions in Porter's story, Strachey's deployment of metaphor, anaphora, and alliteration sacrifices credibility to pyrotechnic display.

Just as Virginia Woolf's private meditations on biography differ from her published assessment, so her letters about *Queen Victoria* register a low opinion that she took pains not to make public. Quite the contrary: in 'The Art of Biography', the essay I began by quoting, she compares Strachey to Boswell in terms that exalt the biographer over the subject: *Queen Victoria*, Woolf claims, 'is a life which, very possibly, will do for the old Queen what Boswell did for the old dictionary maker.' Implicit in this judgement is the premiss that a *Life* has the power to define and even displace a life: 'In time to come Lytton Strachey's Queen Victoria will be Queen Victoria, just as Boswell's Johnson is now

---

[16] Michael Holroyd, *Lytton Strachey: The Years of Achievement 1910–1932* (New York: Holt, Rinehart and Winston, 1968), 431.

Dr. Johnson.'[17] Woolf's confident assessment and others like it
help to explain the animus that has been directed against both
biographies. The attacks on Boswell's *Life* in particular testify
to a deep resentment of the biography's imaginative hold over
generations of readers. Such attacks are motivated as well by a
fear that those who meet Johnson through Boswell do not go
on to a first-hand encounter—that 'the old dictionary maker'
pre-empts a more complex and vital figure.

During the past four decades the bill of indictment has grown
more extensive and more specific. The chief prosecuting attor-
ney, Donald Greene, argues that Boswell's *Life* is not a biography at all but rather a loose-jointed 'assemblage' that deserves
to be 'repealed'.[18] Greene's polemics, always vehement and frequently shrill, do his cause no service; this is especially the case
when he slides from criticism of the work into *ad hominem* attacks
on the author. Yet if we look beneath the rebarbative surface we
find several points that, soberly investigated, advance the conversation about biography in general and Boswell's achievement
in particular.

In Greene's view the *Life* is irreparably damaged by five
cardinal defects. The first is its failure to do justice to the subtle-
ties of Johnson's literary criticism, his political thought, and his

[17] Woolf, *The Death of the Moth and Other Essays*, 191.
[18] A list of Greene's frequent animadversions on Boswell appears in the bibliography appended to Paul J. Korshin and Robert R. Allen (eds.), *Greene Centennial
Studies* (Charlottesville: Univ. Press of Virginia, 1984), 458–68. Two essays in particular contain the gist of his critique. The first is 'Reflections on a Literary Anniversary', *Queen's Quarterly*, 70 (1963), 193–208; this was reprinted in abridged form
in James L. Clifford (ed.), *Twentieth-Century Interpretations of Boswell's Life of Johnson*
(Englewood Cliffs, NJ: Prentice-Hall, 1970), 97–103. The second is ''Tis a Pretty
Book, Mr. Boswell, But—', *Georgia Review*, 32 (1978), 17–43. This was reprinted in
expanded form in John A. Vance (ed.), *Boswell's 'Life of Johnson': New Questions, New
Answers* (Athens: Univ. of Georgia Press, 1985), 110–46. All quotations come from
the later version; citations appear parenthetically in the text.

religious convictions. The second is the absence through long stretches of 'any sort of connected biographical narrative'; by this Greene means the biography's skewed proportions (approximately five-sixths of the text devoted to Johnson in middle and old age) and its liberal offering of letters and other primary sources. The third is a promiscuous inclusiveness that reflects multiple 'breaches of the criteria of discrimination and relevance' (p. 123). The fourth is Boswell's reliance on his 'dreary' journals, which promotes an egotistical emphasis on the biographer's petty and distracting preoccupations. The fifth is a mechanical structure that results from 'component parts' such as blocks of letters 'perfunctorily strung together' (p. 122). In Greene's judgement 'whatever artistry Boswell contributed to the *Life* consist[s] in' the journals alone—and even Johnson's table talk is suspect, given the ways in which Boswell 'add[s] color' and 'heighten[s] . . . dramatic effect' (p. 126). Greene's final verdict is that no 'sane modern scholar' would ever rely upon the *Life* (p. 127).

Underpinning these criticisms is a conviction that biography belongs exclusively to the domain of history and the genre of chronicle. 'Artistry' for Greene is a highly suspect word, for it suggests tampering, manipulation, even dishonesty. Accordingly Boswell's choices amount to 'fabrication'—a revealing word, for it simultaneously recognizes and repudiates the biographer's role as manufacturer. In a riposte to Marshall Waingrow, the pioneering editor of the *Life* manuscript, Greene compares the fabrications of Boswell to those of Shakespeare:

Marshall Waingrow concludes the introduction to his fine edition of Boswell's *Correspondence* relating to the making of the *Life*, 'No matter how many new facts are brought to light, Samuel Johnson will always be somebody's hypothesis, and none has pleased so many, or so long, as Boswell's.' Let researchers into the history of fifteenth-century England take heed, and cease their futile labors: no matter how many new facts about him they bring to light, no Richard III is likely to please so many or for so long as Shakespeare's.[19]

This confused analogy betrays Greene's wish to have it both ways: on the one hand, the *Life* is not a biography but a mere assemblage that could and should be dismantled; on the other hand, the *Life* is a biography, a work of architecture, that compels disbelief to the degree that it exhibits elements of design. Underlying both characterizations is a powerful urge to banish poets from the biographical republic.

More moderate voices have also done their part to misdescribe, simplify, and depreciate. As discerning a scholar as R. W. Chapman claims that 'the finished *Life* is substantially the same thing as the contemporary records. The revision . . . appears as an operation of polishing, not as a structural synthesis.' [20] In a learned and insightful overview of the western biographical tradition, Marc Fumaroli compares Boswell's *Johnson* to Aubrey's *Brief Lives* and Herodotus' *Histories* in terms that perpetuate the stereotypes of all three: colourful grab bags stuffed to bursting with miscellaneous information by resourceful but credulous compilers.[21] Even Adam Sisman, one of the most sensitive students of Boswell's biographical method, helps to perpetuate such stereotypes by combining praise with condescension: 'His artistry', Sisman writes, 'concealed the extent of his invention. The naïveté he betrayed reinforced the sense of authenticity he wished to convey.' [22] The second sentence takes away what the first bestows, the accolade of artistry. In fact Boswell did not

---

[19] Greene, 'Introduction' to *The Politics of Samuel Johnson*, 2nd edn. (Athens: Univ. of Georgia Press, 1990), p. lxii.

[20] Quoted in Waingrow, p. xxii.

[21] Fumaroli, 'Des "Vies" à la biographie: le crépuscule du Parnasse', *Diogène*, 139 (1987), 28.

[22] Sisman, *Boswell's Presumptuous Task* (London: Hamish Hamilton, 2000), 150.

'betray naïveté'—he calculated it for specific rhetorical ends, working intuitively but not naively.

By the end of these chapters I will hope to have convinced you, at the very least, that the belittlement of Boswell is unwarranted. The biographer that emerges from close study of the primary sources is not the Boswell of Greene and Co., 'a tired and timid man, with little talent for organization . . . clinging desperately to the rock of chronological order', but rather a bold, imaginative, and scrupulous artist.[23] My most difficult task is to reach those who believe that biographical truth is found, not made, and that when Fiction marries Fact their bastard child deserves its bend sinister. What I would ask at this stage is no more than a willing suspension of disbelief, which will allow me to argue the case for 'literary form in factual narrative'. I take this phrase from the title of an essay by Ralph W. Rader, the single most important study of the structural principles that shape the *Life of Johnson*.[24] In this essay Rader uncovers 'the creative secret of Boswell's art', the fact that the biographer had 'within his mind not a series of disjunctive photographic impressions but a single dynamic image of Johnson' (p. 7). This image constitutes 'the selective, constructive, and controlling principle of the *Life*, the omnipresent element which vivifies and is made vivid in the whole' (p. 9). Rader argues convincingly that the biography does not tell the protagonist's story as much as it displays his character— a character that is 'infinitely varied but always single' (p. 9). Boswell's commitment to constructing and displaying his image of Johnson, in all its multi-faceted unity, explains the biography's

[23] Greene, ' 'Tis a Pretty Book, Mr. Boswell, But—', 122.

[24] Rader, 'Literary Form in Factual Narrative: The Example of Boswell's *Johnson*', in Philip B. Daghlian (ed.), *Essays in Eighteenth-Century Biography* (Bloomington: Indiana Univ. Press, 1968), 3–42. Reprinted in Vance (ed.), *Boswell's 'Life of Johnson': New Questions, New Answers*, 25–52. I quote from the earlier, longer version; citations appear parenthetically in the text.

lack of suspense, of development, and of narrative momentum, as well as its repeated hatching in of characterizing detail. Rader's provocative approach invites us to compare the experience of reading the *Life* to that of studying a complex work of sculpture, which remains immobile but reveals new dimensions as we examine it from multiple angles and in differing lights.

This ground-breaking essay promotes an understanding of the *Life* as static, quasi-visual construction. In an analysis that builds upon Rader's insights, Paul Alkon attends not only to the static but also to the kinetic features of the biography. His 'Boswellian Time' investigates the ways in which Boswell creates and manipulates the reader's sense of temporal flow—emphasizing duration in order to impart the experience of living through Johnson's life along with him, but also decelerating time in order to underline certain paradigmatic encounters. As part of his study of time in the biography, Alkon examines the consequences of Boswell's theatrical model: 'By describing events as divided into "scenes," Boswell turns emphasis away from analogies involving the static spatial arts of painting, architecture, and embalming to what is a closer and more accurate comparison with the temporal art of drama.'[25] Here Alkon, for all the acuity of his insights, draws an unsustainable distinction between the static and the kinetic: as we will be observing, Boswell combines the model of portrait with the model of drama to achieve an unusual kind of vividness.

Neither critics as persistent as Greene nor admirers as discerning as Rader and Alkon have fully understood how the *Life* was designed to work upon them. Boswell himself is partly to blame: throughout the biography he directs attention away from artistry to industry, from creative choices to dedicated researches. Yet his working manuscript, one of the twentieth century's greatest literary discoveries, tells a much different tale. To explore this

---

[25] Alkon, 'Boswellian Time', in *Studies in Burke and his Time*, 14 (1973), 244–5.

textual labyrinth is to grasp the pervasive fact, the impressive scope, and the intricate nature of those calculations that Boswell took pains to conceal. It is to credit him, in short, with both fidelity and finesse. Because I am committed to assessing the *Life* not only as product but also as process, I take full advantage of the entire archive: Boswell's notes, journals, letters, and proofs, as well as the manuscript itself. My goal is a more subtle, more vital assessment of Boswell the designer—and an enhanced awareness of biography's power to make life into art.

The first chapter explores the close connection between Boswell's biographical goals, his compositional methods, and the production of the first edition. It traces the development of the biography from first draft through cancellanda, paying special attention to the printing-house personnel who played an unusually active role in the shaping of the text. Because of the tangled state of printer's copy, and the fact that Boswell did not consistently read proof against manuscript, the compositors and the corrector became collaborators, whose choices frequently altered what appear to have been Boswell's intentions. The result is a text that challenges us to rethink what D. F. McKenzie has called 'the study of printing history' and Jerome McGann 'the social construction of meaning'.

The second and third chapters analyse those paradigms, the naturalistic portrait and the theatrical conversation-piece, that give the *Life* its distinctive form. In 'Representing Johnson', I argue that Boswell employed every means at his disposal to etch an indelible 'Flemish picture' of his protagonist. The history of the frontispiece, the spacing of the cameo portraits, the reworking of the final character: all these illustrate the importance of display. From the outset the biographer labours to impart his vision by inviting the reader to join him in a sustained act of looking—an act that culminates in the encounter with a Johnson who is brought back to life in the concluding pages. The final verb in the biography sums up these image-making tactics: we can only 'regard' Johnson if we have learned to 'regard' him.[26]

Boswell's pictorial enterprise, which involves slowing down or even suspending temporal flow, coexists with the impulse to structure the biography into a series of playlets. In 'Dramatizing Johnson' I investigate the role of conversation in the *Life*, beginning with exchanges between two or three interlocutors and progressing to such virtuoso set-pieces as the rendering of Johnson's first meeting with Wilkes. In every case the manuscript reveals how adroitly Boswell turned talk into text, devising dramatic structures that impel the reader to 'live o'er each scene' of Johnson's life. At times, indeed, the *Life* becomes something close to a script for performance, fostering thereby the illusion of unmediated access to the protagonist and other *dramatis personae*.

The same commitment to vivid re-creation of Johnson's presence helps to explain the care with which Boswell selected, edited, and positioned his epistolary evidence. The fourth chapter, 'Transmitting Johnson', argues that the prevalence of letters in the *Life*, far from disrupting the narrative or weakening Boswell's authority, enhances the goal of 'illustration'. Johnson's own letters instil a sense of His Master's Voice in its many tonalities, whereas selections from an epistolary exchange function as analogues to or substitutes for actual conversation: Boswell recounts Johnson's last summer, for example, through an artful sequence that taps into multiple correspondences. As with the conversational playlets, we strengthen our admiration of Johnson's extraordinary variety and consistency through a

---

[26] In the first edition the final sentence reads: 'His piety was constant, and was the ruling principle of all his conduct; and the more we consider his character, we shall be the more disposed to regard him with admiration and reverence' (1791, ii. 588). Cf. pp. 78–9 below.

species of stylized eavesdropping—eavesdropping that immerses us in the rhythms, inflexions, and preoccupations of private talk. The final chapter addresses the complex relationship between biographical aesthetics and biographical ethics: at what point does 'high selection' shade into low suppression? The manuscript of the *Life* testifies to the process by which Boswell fashioned a heroic protagonist out of conflicting, ambiguous, and sometimes even repellent testimony. 'Taming Johnson' uncovers the pentimenti within Boswell's portrait. It concentrates on the making of the frontispiece and on passages relating to Johnson's fear of death, his social aggression, his political beliefs, and his sexuality. Boswell's handling of these sensitive subjects highlights both his innovative methods and the importance of placing the finished *Life* (the product) within the context of the biographical workshop (the process).

All five chapters are linked by a commitment to complicating Virginia Woolf's distinction between art and craft and to confounding her prediction that '[biographical] creations are not destined for the immortality which the artist now and then achieves for his creations.'[27] I cannot hope to win over those who believe that every creditable biographer shuns 'literary form in factual narrative', lest a pre-existing truth to life be compromised. I do aspire, however, to overturning for good the stereotype of Boswell the 'tired and timid' hack: if we know where and how to look, his great ambition and his creative intuition are to be found throughout the archive. To redirect the words of King Alfred—whose life, as we know from Boswell, Johnson considered writing—*her mon mæg giet gesion hiora swæth*.[28]

---

[27] Woolf, *The Death of the Moth and Other Essays*, 195–6.

[28] 'Here one can still see their footprints': Alfred, preface to his translation of Gregory the Great's *Cura Pastoralis*, in *Sweet's Anglo-Saxon Reader*, rev. Dorothy Whitelock (Oxford: Clarendon Press, 1975), 6. For Johnson's intention, see *Life* i. 177.

I

Imprinting Johnson

James Boswell's publisher, Edward Dilly, was hot off the mark: the day after news of Johnson's death reached Boswell in December 1784, he received 'a letter from Mr. Dilly mentioning it, and in the true spirit of *the trade* wanting to know if I could have an octavo volume of 400 pages of [Johnson's] conversations ready' within two months.[1] In his reply to Dilly, Boswell insisted that he would write the biography 'deliberately', but that in the meantime he could offer 'my tour with Dr. Johnson, a good Prelude to my large Work his *Life*'.[2] Boswell did indeed proceed 'deliberately': not until the summer of 1786 did he sit down to write; not until the winter of 1790 did printing begin; not until the spring of 1791 did the *Life* appear. That during this six-year period 'my large Work' had become 'my Magnum Opus', had expanded into a prose epic challenging comparison with Gibbon's *Decline and Fall*, is only one reason for this long period of gestation.[3] Part of the 'largeness' of Boswell's enterprise derived from the challenge of imprinting Johnson—Johnson his complex subject and *Johnson* the ambitious work that would bring that subject to life.

In this first stage of our enquiry into Boswell's biographical designs, we will be uncovering the close connection between two senses of 'imprint' as it is defined in Johnson's *Dictionary*: 'to stamp words upon paper by the use of types' and 'to fix on the

---

[1] *Boswell: The Applause of the Jury 1782–1785*, ed. Irma S. Lustig and Frederick A. Pottle (New York: McGraw-Hill, 1981), 272 (18 Dec. 1784).

[2] Waingrow, p. li (23 Dec. 1784).

[3] On 5 Mar. 1789 Boswell wrote to Temple, 'I have the pleasure to tell you, that a part of my Magnum Opus is now ready for the press' (Waingrow, p. lix).

mind or memory'. To analyse the writing, printing, and proofing of the *Life* is to grasp how intimately the first sense is bound
up with the second. My fundamental claim implicates biography with bibliography: the circumstances that surrounded
'imprinting', as a bibliographer would reconstruct it, reflected
and conditioned the circumstances that guided 'imprinting', as
a biographer would devise it. In order to understand both kinds
of 'imprinting', we need to understand the nature of the manuscript, the character (and characters) of the printing house, and
the stages by which the text took shape. As D. F. McKenzie
reminds us, our word 'text' derives from the Latin verb *texere*
'to weave', which is cognate, philologists suggest, with the Greek
techne.[4] At the outset, we will be watching Boswell weave his
web and practise his *techne* in close collaboration with fellow
technologists.

Let us begin with the weaver's distinctive method. In order
to facilitate 'imprinting' of both kinds, Boswell created quarto
leaves by taking folio sheets and folding them once; these folded
sheets were nestled together to produce quires. On one side of
each quarto leaf, he drafted his narrative; the verso of the preceding leaf was reserved for additions or corrections (Figs. 1, 2).
This method served the needs of the compositor, who would not
need to turn over a leaf as he set a given passage in type: rather he
could move back and forth uninterruptedly between the master
text on the recto and the additions and corrections on the facing
verso. This method also served Boswell's compositional habits
and needs: it gave him maximum opportunity for adding and
refining the details that would fix Johnson upon the reader's
mind.

---

[4] D. F. McKenzie, *Bibliography and the Sociology of Texts: The Panizzi Lectures, 1985*
(London: The British Library, 1986), 5–6. (2nd edn. Cambridge University Press,
1999). I quote in every case from the 1st edition.

The quarto leaves of the master manuscript are numbered 1–1046, though there are several gaps in the sequence. However, Boswell almost doubled the length of his text by incorporating into it what he called 'Papers Apart'; these included letters, copies of letters, memoranda, sections of his journal, and a variety of printed sources. At times, a 'Paper Apart' was linked to a 'sub-Paper Apart' and even on occasion to a 'sub-sub-Paper Apart'. Through sigla, abbreviations, and explicit directives (e.g. 'Take in Paper Apart RC'), Boswell cued the compositor to leave the manuscript, absorb the supplementary material, and return to the manuscript.

This method of composition offered one clear advantage to an author pressed for time: it minimized the task of transcribing documents, a task that would be necessary to produce a seamless fair copy. For the same reason, Boswell made all his changes to the first draft directly onto the original quarto leaves. These changes, which often reflect multiple stages of revision, spread densely over both recto and facing verso. As a result, the manuscript resembles a palimpsest, with textual layers superimposed; further layering often occurred when a passage was linked to one or more 'Papers Apart'. Yet this palimpsest also served as printer's copy—witness the signature marks, which correspond to the first edition (Fig. 3), and the notations in the hand of both compositor and corrector.[5]

In short, Boswell gives with one hand and takes away with another: having assisted the compositor by writing on recto and revising on facing verso, Boswell made his task much more difficult by handing him the foulest of foul papers. Moreover, he continued to rewrite through two sets of proof: first proof (a

---

[5] Marion S. Pottle, Claude Colleer Abbott, and Frederick A. Pottle, *Catalogue of the Papers of James Boswell at Yale University*, 3 vols. (Edinburgh: Edinburgh Univ. Press and Yale Univ. Press, 1993), i. 85–7.

partial set of which has been recovered) and revised proof (which has survived in its entirety). Beginning with the first draft and ending with stop-press corrections, certain sections of the *Life* undergo more than five stages of revision. Boswell proudly compares his biography to the *Odyssey*; it is therefore doubly appropriate that it should constitute, along with Joyce's *Ulysses*, the pre-eminent example in British literature of a 'many-layered and highly complex text that carries the dynamics of an extended textual development within it'.[6]

Boswell launched his epic enterprise in July 1786 with an act of quasi-monastic *askesis*: 'These three days I confined myself to the house and took only tea and dry toast to breakfast and boiled milk and dry toast at night, and this discipline made me quiet, and I did the first part of Dr. Johnson's *Life* and made arrangements for more of it.'[7] But protracted self-discipline was not Boswell's forte, to put it mildly. It is likely that the 'great Work' would have foundered without the steady hand and inspiring example of Edmond Malone, who was himself engaged on a *magnum opus*, his pioneering edition of Shakespeare. Like a good teacher, Malone mingled criticism and exhortation with ingenious incentives. He drew attention to 'colloquialisms and vulgarisms of all sorts'.[8] He advised Boswell to 'condense as much as possible, always preserving perspicuity'.[9] Most importantly, perhaps, Malone gave Boswell the confidence he needed to keep on going: 'We revised a part of [the *Life*], which he thought well of, and dispelled my vaporish diffidence; and he surprised me . . . with a page of it on two different types, that we might settle how it was to be printed.'[10] For reasons that also combined the experi-

---

[6] *Life* i. 12; Hans Walter Gabler, *Ulysses: A Critical and Synoptic Edition* (New York: Garland, 1984), 1895.

[7] *Boswell: The English Experiment 1785–1789*, ed. Irma S. Lustig and Frederick A. Pottle (New York: McGraw-Hill, 1986), 81–2 (9–11 July 1786).

[8] Baker, 387.   [9] Ibid.   [10] *English Experiment*, 96–7 (7 Nov. 1786).

mental with the inspirational, a trial proof of the title-page was printed almost a year before the biography was ready to go to press (see Fig. 5). From early in the compositional process, therefore, Boswell and his principal adviser had in view what French historians of the book have taught us to call *mise en page*—the visual display of text and the interplay between typography and content.[11]

Yet preliminary experiments with type could not disguise the fact that a marathon stretched ahead—a marathon that combined writing with rewriting. As Boswell told his old friend William Johnson Temple, 'Whenever I have completed the rough draught, by which I mean the Work without nice correction, Malone and I are to prepare one half perfectly, and then it goes to press.'[12] In the event, however, Boswell and Malone began to revise before the rough draft was finished; in fact Boswell did not complete the biography until March 1791, when most of it had advanced to the stage of revised proof.[13] When 'nice correction' started in October 1789, the two men 'precisely reversed the procedure they had followed in revising the *Tour*': as Peter Baker notes, 'this time Boswell read aloud to Malone and entered most of the revisions in his own hand. From the manuscript, then, we cannot tell who suggested what changes.'[14]

---

[11] For an incisive discussion of this topic, see two essays in *Buch und Buchhandel in Europa im achtzehnten Jahrhundert: fünftes Wolfenbütteler Symposium 1977* (Hamburg: Wolfenbütteler Schriften zur Geschichte des Buchwesens 4, 1981): D. F. McKenzie, 'Typography and Meaning: The Case of William Congreve' (81–125) and Nicolas Barker, 'Typography and the Meaning of Words: The Revolution in the Layout of Books in the Eighteenth Century' (126–65).

[12] Waingrow, p. lix (10 Jan. 1789).

[13] Boswell wrote to his son Alexander on 14 Mar. 1791: 'I am now *writing* the *last sheet* of my Book. But the whole, including Dedication and Table of contents will not I imagine be all *printed* sooner than this day fortnight' (ibid., p. lxvi).

[14] Baker, 178.

This is not the case for the proof sheets, many of which Malone annotated. Nevertheless, it is important to recognize that, after Malone left for Ireland in late 1790, Boswell completed both the writing and the proofing of the biography with only minimal assistance from afar. *Il miglior fabbro* had fulfilled his most important function.

If Malone merits the title his modern biographer has bestowed upon him, 'midwife to Boswell's *Life of Johnson*',[15] then the printing-house personnel—those who actually delivered the book—deserve almost equal praise for bringing about a happy issue. Their roles can be reconstructed from notations on the manuscript, comments and queries on both sets of proof, and Boswell's journal and correspondence. Two of the five principals, the master printer and the indexer, led lives that are documented elsewhere in the historical record. Thanks to the Boswell archive alone, the three others emerge tenuously out of 'the dead Night of the Past', through which the *Life of Johnson*, according to Carlyle, flings 'a little row of Naphtha-lamps'. The light from these lamps, which extends further than Carlyle could have realized, allows us to rescue the two compositors and the corrector of the *Life* from 'boundless dark Oblivion'.[16] But only just, for the record is as scant as it is vivid.

Of those whose *techne* supported Boswell's, Henry Baldwin, one of eighteenth-century London's most important printers, takes a special sort of precedence.[17] On 1 January 1790 Boswell 'delivered the Introduction of [the *Life*] to Baldwin, that I might

[15] Peter Martin, *Edmond Malone: Shakespearean Scholar* (Cambridge: Cambridge Univ. Press, 1995), 144.

[16] Thomas Carlyle, 'Boswell's Life of Johnson', in *Critical and Miscellaneous Essays*, vol. iii (Centenary Edition, ed. H. D. Traill, London: Chapman and Hall, 1899), 80.

[17] The most helpful profile is to be found in Ian Maxted, *The London Book Trades 1775–1800* (London: Dawson, 1977), 10.

say my book was *at* if not *in* the press on New Year's Day. The honest, friendly printer was a little gruff about my mode of carrying on the work, but I made allowance for him.'[18] This journal entry, which struggles for a tone of jaunty confidence, epitomizes the strong but equivocal ties linking author to printer. Baldwin's 'gruff' behaviour reflects the fact that Boswell, who had already borrowed substantial sums from him, was asking Baldwin to participate in a legal fiction and to take a financial gamble: printer's copy was not yet delivered, even when delivered it would not be complete, and Boswell's unorthodox 'mode of carrying on the work' risked tying up the resources of the press for an indefinite period. On the other hand, Boswell was a shareholder in Baldwin's *London Magazine*; Baldwin had profited from the two editions of the *Tour to the Hebrides*; and he stood to make an even greater profit, both material and immaterial, from a successful biography. Moreover, Boswell had become an *ami de la maison*, dropping in for dinner and tea at Baldwin's 'hospitable table'.[19] Boswell's nervous condescension reflects the fact that he depended upon a tradesman to sustain his enterprise and salvage his reputation: for the past two and a half years he had been struggling to complete his recalcitrant biography, claiming all the while that the 'Great Work' was about to go to press. For both men, various kinds of credit were at stake.

In his ambitious recent study *The Nature of the Book*, Adrian Johns questions the concept of a fixed and standardized 'print culture', a concept that has permeated the field of book history for the past several decades. From Johns's revisionist perspective, books in the early modern period did not possess an aura of immutable authority. Quite the contrary: in 'a culture characterized by nothing so much as indeterminacy', they were

---

[18] *Great Biographer*, 27.
[19] Ibid. 225; cf. pp. 106, 123.

widely perceived as unreliable.[20] Accordingly, authors, printers, and booksellers needed to find ways of inspiring trust in sceptical readers, who 'judged the printed books they met by what they knew of the people, places, and practices implicated in their production, distribution, and use'.[21]

Johns's investigation of 'the techniques . . . by which books could be appraised and accredited' helps us to think freshly about the making and marketing of the *Life of Johnson*.[22] In particular, it focuses our attention on the advertisement to the second edition, which speaks across the complete span of the project to the interlocking ambitions and anxieties we have just been considering. In this advertisement, Boswell simultaneously 'accredits' his own enterprise and Baldwin's. After trumpeting the success of the first edition, he stresses his continuing endeavours to 'rectify some mistakes, and to enrich the Work with many valuable additions', thanks to the cooperation 'not only of some of my particular friends, but of many other learned and ingenious men'. He eulogizes the dedicatee, Sir Joshua Reynolds, who gave 'the strongest testimony to [the work's] fidelity'. And he makes special mention of the printer: 'May I be permitted to say that the typography of both editions does honour to the press of Mr. *Henry Baldwin*, now Master of the Worshipful Company of Stationers, whom I have long known as a worthy man and an obliging friend' (*Life* i. 10). The President of the Royal Academy vouches for the biography's contents, contents enhanced by the cognoscenti and ushered into the world twice over by the Stationer of Stationers—in the words of the title-page, 'printed by Henry Baldwin'. Never was trust-by-association more powerfully urged.

---

[20] Adrian Johns, *The Nature of the Book: Print and Knowledge in the Making* (Chicago: Univ. of Chicago Press, 1998), 36.
[21] Ibid. 188.   [22] Ibid. 37.

By 'typography' Boswell appears to mean 'the settling and arrangement of types and printing from them . . . hence, the arrangement and appearance of printed matter' (the *OED*'s second definition). Baldwin did indeed play an important role in the 'settling' of type for the first edition, but the publisher Edward Dilly, Malone, and John Nichols (printer and editor of the *Gentleman's Magazine*) also influenced the deliberations. It was Baldwin who started the process by arranging for a preliminary casting off and by making suggestions about format, type, and paper: according to Baldwin's calculations, 'by using a *pica* instead of an *English* letter in printing my book, I might comprise it within such a number of sheets as a guinea-volume should contain, which I could not do in English letter unless upon a *medium* instead of a *demy* paper, so as to have a larger page.'[23] The gist of Baldwin's suggestion is that, if the type were diminished in size by shifting from English (with a body-size of approximately 92 mm) to pica (approximately 81 mm), then the biography could be comprised within a single volume priced at one guinea; adherence to English text type would necessitate an increase in paper size.[24] Two days later, Boswell visited the printing house, where he learned that 'from the computation of my manuscript, or *copy* as it is called, there were 416,000 words, which we averaged would make too many pages in quarto even upon *pica*, and therefore it was thought by Baldwin that I should make two quarto volumes on *English* and sell them at thirty shillings'.[25]

Yet Boswell persisted in his wish that the biography might appear as a single volume. Given its length, however, this would necessitate a change in format from quarto to folio. At this point

[23] *Great Biographer*, 30 (9 Jan. 1790).
[24] See the tables in Philip Gaskell, *A New Introduction to Bibliography* (New York: Oxford Univ. Press, 1972), 15, 73–5.
[25] *Great Biographer*, 31 (11 Jan. 1790).

Malone intervened, telling Boswell that 'I might as well throw it into the Thames, for a folio would not now be read.' Malone went on to propose an alternative: 'His scheme was to print 1,000 on pica in quarto, in one volume however thick, and at the same time by *overrunning* the types, as it is called, to print 1,000 in octavo, which would be kept *in petto* and be in readiness for sale whenever the quarto was sold.'[26] Had this 'scheme' been adopted, the type would have been kept standing and then have been imposed for an octavo reprint. As precedent and parallel, Malone may have had in mind John Taylor's edition of Demosthenes, which had been published by Cambridge University Press in octavo by overrunning the types of the original quarto edition.[27] But canny as Malone's proposal sounded, it was rejected by John Nichols for several reasons:

In the first place, by *over-running* I saved only £25 upon a hundred sheets, nothing being saved but the half of the compositor' payment. . . . In the second place, my octavo edition would have all the errors of the quarto;[28] and thirdly, it would hurt the sale of my quarto, as its being ready would be known. He advised me rather to print 1,500 in quarto, and assured me that I would run no risk of not disposing of that number.[29]

Nichols's advice carried the day. During the initial stages of printing, Boswell continued to hope that it would be possible 'to confine [the biography] within one quarto volume though it should be a very thick one', but by August 1790, with the page count approaching 500 and more than half the manuscript left to set, it became clear that two volumes would be necessary.[30]

[26] *Great Biographer*, 32–3 (13 Jan. 1790).

[27] Gaskell, *New Introduction to Bibliography*, 117.

[28] By an 'edition' Boswell means what modern bibliographers would call an 'issue'.

[29] *Great Biographer*, 33.

[30] Waingrow, pp. lxiii–lxiv.

However, the purchase price was increased from thirty shillings to two guineas, and the print run from 1500 to 1750.[31] Nichols's prediction was accurate: all the non-presentation copies of the first edition were sold by the end of 1792.

That casting off could be performed at all is a minor miracle, given the unfinished and heavily revised state of the manuscript, as well as the large and miscellaneous category of 'Papers Apart'. But casting off copy such as Boswell's was perhaps the least of the skills required by the compositor, a certain 'Mr. Plymsell', whose Christian name has not entered the range of the naphtha lamps.[32] Boswell, who describes Plymsell as 'an intelligent and accurate man', improvises a fragmentary but revealing tribute to him in one of the 'Boswelliana': 'The compositor following my perplexed [steps>] writing better than I could do myself. . . . The Stag cannot trace his own doublings. The sagacious hound can find out and follow them all.'[33] Dogging Boswell's steps and tracing his doublings, Plymsell admirably fulfilled Joseph Moxon's charge to 'get himself into the meaning of the *Author*' and to take pains not to let 'such Work to go out of his Hands as may bring Scandal upon himself, and Scandal and prejudice upon the *Master Printer*'.[34] As Moxon stipulates, '*it is necessary that a* Composition *be a good English Schollar at least; and that he know the present traditional* Spelling *of all English Words, and that he have so much Sence and Reason, as to* Point *his Sentences properly*'.[35] Though a

---

[31] *Literary Career*, 155; *Waingrow*, p. lxviii (to Andrew Erskine, 6 Mar. 1793).

[32] It was usually the compositor and not the printer who was responsible for casting off (Gaskell, *New Introduction to Bibliography*, 41). On a Paper Apart for MS 37, the compositor signed his name 'J. Plymsell'. He may have been the 'John Plymsell' listed in Maxted, *London Book Trades*, 178.

[33] *Great Biographer*, 62 (14 June 1790); *Boswelliana* M54 (datable to 1790).

[34] Joseph Moxon, *Mechanick Exercises on the Whole Art of Printing*, ed. Herbert Davis and Harry Carter, 2nd edn. (London: Oxford Univ. Press, 1962), 212, 219. [35] Ibid. 193.

comment by Boswell on one of the revises suggests that he considered himself responsible for 'pointing',[36] the proof sheets show
that Plymsell fulfilled Moxon's charge and more.

Even Moxon, however, could not have foreseen all the challenges faced by the compositor in this case. Perhaps the most
unusual of these challenges derived from Boswell's habit of inter-
lining alternative words or phrases as he drafted a given passage,
but then forgetting to return and indicate his final choice. To
choose one example: Boswell, mentioning the spare room that
Johnson had set aside for him, writes first that he 'took possession
of it', and then indicates an alternative, 'made trial of it'; both
formulations are allowed to stand (*Life MS* ii. 168). By the time
of revises, 'took possession' had been chosen. But who made the
choice? It may have been Boswell, who at certain stages of the
long printing process visited Baldwin's quite frequently. But it
is impossible that he himself should have resolved more than a
fraction of the unresolved alternatives. The task must therefore
have fallen, more often than not, to Mr Plymsell, who may have
turned to the corrector for guidance (as did the compositor of
Boswell's *Tour to the Hebrides*).

In addition, Mr Plymsell had to confront the challenge of
ambiguous changes, as when Boswell originally wrote 'the
perfect propriety of his private conduct', interlined 'uniform'
between 'the' and 'perfect', and then neglected to delete 'perfect'; the compositor resolved this problem by setting both 'perfect' and 'uniform' (*Life MS* i. 262). Moreover, he had often to
untangle a textual snarl caused by changes of such intricacy and
scope that they required a well-nigh heroic ability to 'get . . . into
the meaning of the *Author*'. Under such circumstances, it is no

---

[36] 'You do not put a semicolon often enough. Pray attend to this. But it is *my
duty* to point. So I have no right to find fault' (revised proof, ii. 217, Hyde Collection).

wonder that even Mr Plymsell made mistakes, some of which yielded sentences that have earned Boswell praise he does not fully deserve.[37] For these reasons, the *Life* might well be judged a collaborative text, one that emerges out of a sustained negotiation between author and printing house. And Mr Plymsell in particular deserves recognition not only for sustaining the credit of his author and his employer, but also for making a creative contribution to the masterpiece he helped to bring into the world.

For five months, from the beginning of September 1790 until the end of January 1791, Mr Plymsell was assisted by another compositor, whom Baldwin hired when Boswell was producing copy at a fast clip and then let go when he was working too 'sluggishly' to warrant the expense.[38] In contrast to his oblique, unpublished tribute to Mr Plymsell, Boswell includes in the *Life* a sentence explicitly praising this second compositor, whose family name was 'Manning': 'a decent sensible man who had [prin>] composed about one half of his Dictionary when in Mr. Strahan's printing house and a great part of his Lives of the Poets when in Mr. Nichols's Printinghouse and now (in his ____ year) when in Mr. Baldwin's printinghouse has [done>] composed a part of the first edition of this Work concerning him.' Boswell inserts this cameo within an anecdote that is positioned late in the biography. Its inclusion within a Paper Apart called 'Varia', as well as the manuscript reading 'now . . . has composed', furnish an interesting clue to the chronology of composition and revision: the anecdote must have been written during or soon after Manning's five-month stint at Baldwin's.[39] Boswell had to leave a blank in the manuscript for Mr Manning's age,

---

[37] See the discussion in Ch.3 of the sequence that yielded 'buffeting his books'.

[38] Baker, 395.

[39] Paper Apart 'Varia' is cued to MS 966 (June 1784). Cf. *Life* iv. 321.

a blank that is filled in proof with 'seventy-seventh year'. It is tempting to speculate that Boswell asked Manning himself for this information, and told him why he wanted it. One hopes as well that the elderly compositor, veteran of a long career in several of London's most important printing establishments, took pleasure in knowing that his association with both biographer and biographical subject had been rescued from 'boundless dark Oblivion'.

If Baldwin's printing house conformed to the design prescribed by Moxon, then off the compositors' room was a 'little Closet' occupied by the corrector, Mr Selfe.[40] Though he cannot be ranked with such eminent scholar-correctors as Thomas Ruddiman or William Bowyer,[41] Selfe was a well-trained linguist: his queries on the proof sheets of the *Life* make it clear that he knew Greek, Latin, French, and perhaps Italian. He had already done good work for Boswell and Malone, having corrected both first and second editions of the *Tour to the Hebrides* and composed the analytical table of contents for the second. As Malone told Boswell, when urging him in 1785 to give Selfe a bonus, the corrector 'had a great deal of the trouble and the merit in decyphering the MS. [of the *Tour*]; for in all difficulties [the compositor] applied to him'.[42]

Under ordinary circumstances Mr Selfe would have been assisted by a 'reading boy' or 'copy-holder', who as the terms suggest read the copy aloud while the corrector marked up proof.[43] The need for such a check upon the compositor was strongly emphasized by none other than Samuel Richardson, master printer as well as master novelist:

---

[40] *Mechanick Exercises*, ed. Davis and Carter, 247.

[41] Percy Simpson, *Proof-Reading in the Sixteenth Seventeenth and Eighteenth Centuries* (London: Oxford Univ. Press, 1935), 158–9.   [42] Baker, 268.

[43] Simpson, *Proof-Reading*, 136; Gaskell, *New Introduction to Bibliography*, 111–13.

We find a Corrector of the Press necessary, in order to sweep-out . . . the grosser faults of the Compositor, the cleanest of which must make some and often make what they call *Outs* and *Doubles;* that is, *Omissions* of Words and Passages, and *Repetitions* of both, through Inattention. The Corrector of the Press takes Care to make the Proof conformable to the Copy, and to correct Typographical Errors.[44]

Indeed, even the acute Mr Plymsell was guilty of sins of omission and commission; Mr Selfe caught a number of these, witness the 'Out' markings in the manuscript. However, Mr Selfe, who failed to spot many of the compositor's misreadings, was guilty of sins of omission himself. But he should not be severely faulted for these sins. First, it is inconceivable that Mr Selfe had the assistance of a 'copy-holder': no boy, however skilled, could have deciphered Boswell's manuscript with sufficient accuracy and efficiency to have warranted the attempt. Second, given the state of the copy it is probable that the corrector performed his collation by moving from proof sheet to manuscript rather than from manuscript to proof sheet. The result would have been a blurring of discrepancies between manuscript and proof.[45] Third, the corrector's efforts were not regularly supplemented by those of Boswell or Malone.

In his study of the letters by Johnson that appear in the *Life*, R. W. Chapman argues that 'not even Boswell and Malone compared their proofs, word for word, with the originals'.[46] Taking his cue from Chapman, Marshall Waingrow, who has spent decades studying the *Life* manuscript, declares in the introduction to his edition: 'The most important disclosure of

[44] Richardson to William Blackstone, 10 Feb. 1756, in I. G. Philip, *William Blackstone and the Reform of the Oxford University Press in the Eighteenth Century* (Oxford: Oxford Bibliographical Society, 1957), 39.

[45] *Life MS* i, p. xxv n. 1.

[46] *The Letters of Samuel Johnson*, ed. R. W. Chapman, 3 vols. (Oxford: Clarendon Press, 1952), iii. 306.

the proof-sheets is that neither Boswell nor Malone read them against the manuscript.'[47] Such sweeping conclusions, however, may need to be reconsidered. It is undoubtedly the case that copy cannot have been collated with proofs in any *systematic* way: too many errors and inventive compositorial readings remained unnoticed. Nevertheless, one piece of evidence exists to suggest that, at least on occasion, manuscript and proof were compared. This evidence comes in a journal entry for 24 July 1790. After two days of 'social glee', Boswell goes 'to Baldwin's printing-office, where I was happy to find myself again, though I found neither my friend Baldwin the master, Selfe the corrector, nor Plymsell the compositor'. Disconcerted by their absence, Boswell turns for comfort to his publisher Edward Dilly, who plies him 'liberally' with 'old hock'. 'Was warmed', Boswell writes, 'and wished to have a social evening at a coffee-house.' During this 'social evening' his pocket is 'picked of a proof-sheet of my *Life of Johnson*, with the manuscript belonging to it. But this could not be remedied, and luckily all was secured in print but two lines which I could supply.'[48] Unfortunately, we can never learn the facts that would help us to grasp the import of this anecdote: what was the passage in question? who took the initiative in calling for a collation? does this journal entry describe a unique occurrence? We can conclude, however, that first proof of the *Life* comes closer to being an interpretation than a reproduction of Boswell's text, and that this is the case because of striking anomalies in the state of the printer's copy and in the mode of correcting.

As we complete our account of those in the *officina Baldwini* who brought the *Life* to life, we come to the fourth of Boswell's collaborators: the young barrister Thomas Edlyne Tomlins, who

[47] Waingrow, *Life MS* i, p. xxiv.
[48] *Great Biographer*, 95–6. Michael F. Suarez, SJ, draws attention to this entry in his review of *Life MS* i (*TLS*, 15 Dec. 1995, 11–12).

was employed, along with Mr Selfe, as a corrector. It is one measure of his difference from the other three that we know Tomlins's Christian name. Another difference is that employment as a corrector was for Tomlins only a temporary expedient: he returned to the practice of law, entered government service, and went on to achieve a knighthood. But in the early 1790s he was down on his luck. As Boswell, himself a floundering barrister, observes with a note of irony, 'Mr. Tomlins . . . having contracted debt, was obliged to quit the bar, and was now honestly getting his livelihood by *certain* diligence.'[49]

In order to supplement his income as corrector, Tomlins offered to index the *Life*; he also made the ingenious suggestion that the index be prefixed to the biography, thereby bringing the page count of volume i closer to that of volume ii.[50] But Tomlins's most distinctive contribution was the result of an oversight: as we will soon be noting, his uncorrected index entry for Thomas Percy gave away the contents of a cancelled leaf. This mistake, which mortified Percy but may well have secretly delighted Boswell, did nothing to impair the cordial relationship that had developed between the two barristers. In fact 'Counsellor Tomlins', as Boswell called him, was the only one of Baldwin's employees to be included in the dinner celebrating the appearance of the second edition.[51]

Of these five men—Baldwin, Plymsell, Selfe, Manning, and Tomlins—Boswell dealt most closely with Plymsell and Selfe: it was they who laboured in the vineyard from start to finish, bearing the burden across a fifteen-month span. What they thought of the work and its author we can only surmise, though the

[49] *Great Biographer*, 123 (14 Feb. 1791).

[50] Baker, 395. Despite this manœuvre, there was still an imbalance: volume i of the first edition is fifty-two pages shorter than volume ii.

[51] *Great Biographer*, 239 (3 Oct. 1793).

record—consisting of manuscript, annotated proof sheets, journal entries, and correspondence—gets us tantalizingly close to the human reality. As Philip Gaskell eloquently observes, 'the old printers were men, not abstractions, who had good days and bad ones; who got on each other's nerves and lost their tempers; who had moments of disastrous clumsiness; and who improvised and botched without hesitation whenever their tools or materials did not precisely meet the needs of the moment'.[52] Mr Plymsell and Mr Selfe must often have 'improvised': for one thing, the author in question had set them an epic challenge in the form of a long and scarcely legible manuscript that was unfinished and undergoing constant revision, even in the final months of printing. Yet compositor and corrector never 'botched' in any serious sense of the word: even Boswell at his most demanding found comparatively little to fault. The anecdote that includes the brief profile of Mr Manning serves as a foil to his own experience at Baldwin's:

No man was more ready to make an apology when he had censured unjustly, than Johnson. When a proof-sheet of one of his works was brought to him, he found fault with the mode in which a part of it was arranged, refused to read it, and in a passion desired that the compositor might be sent to him. . . . By producing the manuscript, [the compositor] at once satisfied Dr. Johnson that he was not to blame. Upon which Johnson candidly and earnestly said to him, 'Mr. Compositor, I ask your pardon. Mr. Compositor, I ask your pardon, again and again.' (*Life* iv. 321)

The record strongly suggests that nothing like this episode occurred during the printing of the *Life*: Boswell, though passionate about his book, never had cause or inclination to fly into 'a passion'. As R. W. Chapman concluded from his pioneering study of the proofs, 'If [Boswell] betrays a fault, it is nothing less

---

[52] Gaskell, *New Introduction to Bibliography*, 47.

venial than over-anxiety; and if he is over-anxious, it is all in the good cause of accuracy. For the rest, his marginalia show all the virtues that a printer or publisher could wish to find in his author.'[53]

In dealing with Plymsell and Selfe, Boswell tended to be both gracious and demanding. His hortatory politesse is epitomized in a note written ten months after printing had begun: 'This is very well done indeed. Pray gentlemen compositors let me have as much as you can before Christmas.'[54] Good work earned unequivocal praise: 'I am obliged to you for the suggestions. In this page there are two good corrections' (i. 393). But Boswell could be exasperated and even peevish. He does not hesitate to rebuke when last-minute additions are neglected: 'How came you to omit the title of Dr. Dunbar's Book? I sent it on a slip of paper last night' (ii. 323). He reproves what he considers unjustified ignorance: 'Don't you know the *Stephani* the famous Printers!' (ii. 329). He cracks his whip: 'I expected to have seen also the revise of H.h *at least*. I request a little more dispatch' (ii. 225). Yet the exasperated taskmaster must have been exasperating as well. Periods of constant surveillance, when he would visit Baldwin's in order 'to quicken' the printing,[55] alternated with periods of stagnation, when copy dried up. And one wonders what Mr Plymsell thought when Boswell stood over him in the compositors' room, dictating changes to be entered in the copy or resolving stylistic alternatives directly in the type.[56]

---

[53] R. W. Chapman, 'Boswell's Proof-Sheets—I' (*London Mercury*, 15 (1926–7), 50). This essay and its companion, 'Boswell's Proof-Sheets—II', were reprinted as a single essay, 'Boswell's Revises of the Life of Johnson', in *Johnson and Boswell Revised* (Oxford: Clarendon Press, 1928), 21–50.

[54] Revises for vol. ii, 257 of the 1st edition (Hyde Collection). Henceforth references to notes on the revises will appear parenthetically in the text.

[55] Waingrow, p. lxii (2 Feb. 1790).

[56] See, for example, *Life MS* i. 488.

What must have earned the respect of both compositor and corrector was Boswell's devotion to accuracy, his attention to detail, and his awareness of technical difficulties. On an early set of first proof, he writes: 'For Press when carefully read by Mr. Selfe, and corrected. Pray be very attentive, that I may have no cancels and few Errata.'[57] This directive becomes his regular formula: each instalment of proof is headed, 'For press when carefully read by Mr. Selfe and corrected.' Boswell himself read 'carefully', attending to the style of type ('Dr. Adams's words to be in Roman') as well as its size ('Small Caps').[58] He queried the choice of catchwords and scrutinized quotation marks with the care of a devoted copy editor: 'If you mean to put [close quotes] at the end of each paragraph you must not omit it—Do as you will uniformly' (ii. 318). At times he responded to the layout of a page almost as if it were a canvas: looking at the space between the end of 1783 and the beginning of 1784, he directs Plymsell, 'Make a little more White between the years' (ii. 477). Even the positioning of asterisks did not escape him: Mr Plymsell preferred to place the asterisks designating acknowledged works by Johnson before and not after the title in question, but Boswell decreed that to do so 'would appear aukward' (*Life MS* i. 402).

Though he could be somewhat peremptory, Boswell also considered the difficulties his preferences, and in particular his changes, might create for Mr Plymsell. Having added a footnote in revised proof, he tells the compositor: 'I think you may find room for the note, without overrunning by taking *shop* up into the line above' (ii. 186). When he appends information on Mrs Knowles's needlework, he gives Mr Plymsell permission not to incorporate the new passage: 'If the *note* can be printed without deranging the presswork, well—If not, leave it out' (ii. 223).

---

[57] First proof, p. 25 (Hyde Collection).
[58] *Life MS* i. 383, 387.

Some changes had to be made, however, regardless of the dis-
ruption they might cause. Yet Boswell finds a way of softening his
commands by making author and compositor into full-fledged
colleagues: 'I am sorry that there must be a little over-running
etc., in this sheet. But we must make as good a Book as may be'
(i. 161). In the same spirit he tells Mr Plymsell, 'I am not sure
whether there should be a full stop or point of interrogation at
life. Do as you will' (ii. 230).

As scholar-corrector, Mr Selfe was granted a different sort
of latitude. When he noticed that the text of Johnson's Greek
epitaph for Goldsmith was misaccentuated, Selfe suggested to
Boswell, 'Would it not be better to omit [the accents] or make
them right—if you choose to keep them I will take Care of them.'
Boswell gives final responsibility to Selfe: 'I leave it optional to
you to have accents or not. Mr. Thomas Warton used none' (ii.
93). On occasion, Selfe not only corrected, he made or suggested
making certain stylistic changes (ii. 237, ii. 245).[59] One of these
suggestions reveals how acutely the corrector was responding to
Boswell's biographical method, and in particular to his handling
of letters. Mr Selfe's note registers a stylistic concern that shades
into the practical: 'Should there not be an Introduction to this
Letter?—It certainly begins too abrupt[ly] . . . It must be short—
the other side is at Press' (ii. 93). The fact that Boswell rejects this
idea does nothing to diminish the significance of Selfe's willing-
ness to intervene.

In their separate but interlocking ways, then, both compositor and corrector contribute significantly to the imprinting of
Johnson. At the beginning of this chapter, I suggested that the
two enterprises—'stamping words upon paper by the use of
types' and 'fixing on the mind or memory'—were closely allied.
Two examples from the proof sheets will illustrate how Boswell's

[59] See also ibid. 479.

concern for the collegial enterprise at Baldwin's ('*We* must make as good a Book as may be') intersected with his biographical aesthetic. The first example involves a decision to delete in its entirety an anecdote relayed by William Bowles:

The Dr. valued himself a good deal on being able to do every thing for himself. He visited without a servant when he went to stay at the houses of his friends, and found few or no occasions to employ the servants belonging to the family. He knew how to mend his own stockings to darn his linen or to sew on a button on his cloaths. 'I am not (he would often say) an helpless man.'[60]

This homespun vignette does exactly what Johnson calls for in biography: it 'lead[s] the thoughts into domestick privacies, and display[s] the minute details of daily life'.[61] However, when he scrutinizes the revises, Boswell decides that Bowles's report fails to satisfy his most important criterion, that of 'scrupulous authenticity'. Therefore it must go. But even as he instructs Plymsell to remove the passage, Boswell thinks about compensatory moves: 'I doubt this therefore let it go out; and thus you may more easily get in a note to Dr. Burney in the next page' (ii. 464).

A second act of imprinting, or re-imprinting, occurs when Boswell decides to delete on the grounds of hyper-fidelity rather than on those of dubious authenticity. In his account of a dialogue concerning predestination and free will, Boswell had quoted Johnson's endorsement of his view that 'human life was not machinery'; this conversation was provoked by 'the shocking sight of fifteen men executed before Newgate' and by attendant worries about 'a chain of fatality' (*Life* iv. 328–9). In proof Johnson is allowed to offer a further example to counter the belief that all events are 'planned and directed by the Supreme Being': 'The

---

[60] Waingrow, 250.

[61] *The Rambler*, ed. W. J Bate and Albrecht B. Strauss, 3 vols. (New Haven: Yale Univ. Press, 1969), i. 321 (*Rambler* No. 60).

small pox can less be accounted for than an execution, upon the supposition of machinery, for we are sure it comes without a fault' (ii. 522). Boswell's revision substitutes sonorous generality for potentially shocking specificity: 'He agreed with me now, as he always did, upon the great question of the liberty of the human will which has been in all ages perplexed with so much sophistry' (ii. 522). But even as he makes this major change, Boswell gives permission for practical concerns to trump stylistic nuance: 'If you want room *in all ages* may be omitted.' As it turned out, Mr Plymsell was able to find room for 'in all ages', thereby imprinting a softened version of Johnson's philosophical reflections.

This particular change in revised proof makes it clear that certain kinds of plain talk from his protagonist could activate a censoring mechanism in Boswell. The same mechanism triggered one of the six cancels that he ordered during the final period of the book's production.[62] As Boswell tells Malone, both of them had neglected to notice just how unrestrained were some of Johnson's remarks on the sexual behaviour of married couples:

I must have a cancelled leaf in Vol. II of that passage where there is a conversation as to conjugal infidelity on the husband's side, and his wife saying she did not care how many women he went to if he *loved* her alone; with my proposing to mark in a pocket book every time a wife *refuses* etc. etc. I wonder how you and I admitted this to the publick eye for Windham etc. were struck with its *indelicacy* and it might hurt the Book much.[63]

The differences between cancellandum and cancellans illuminate Johnson's thoughts on female sexuality and Boswell's tactics

---

[62] The basic information about the cancels can be found in *Literary Career*, 150–5, and *Life* iv. 555–7. See also Chapman, 'Boswell's Revises of the Life of Johnson', 45–50.　　　　　　　　　　　　　　[63] Baker, 400–1.

for presenting such thoughts. Because we will be exploring these issues in 'Taming Johnson', it suffices at the moment to make two points about this cancel. First, Boswell rarely had occasion to perform radical surgery on his text, especially when such surgery amounted to expurgation. He does so here with reluctance: 'it is however mighty good stuff' is his concluding remark to Malone.[64] Second, it is virtually unprecedented for the highly decorous Malone—the Malone who had scrutinized Boswell's *Tour* with an eagle eye—to pass for publication an instance of marked 'indelicacy'.

Concerns about propriety rather than indelicacy appear to have motivated the cancellation of three names in Boswell's account of a quarrel between Johnson and Topham Beauclerk. This quarrel began when Beauclerk maintained that 'every wise man who intended to shoot himself, took two pistols, that he might be sure of doing it at once'. As supporting examples, Beauclerk referred to two suicides—that of Lord Charles Spencer's cook, who 'shot himself with [only] one pistol, and lived ten days in great agony', and that of a certain 'Mr. Delmis, who loved buttered muffins, but durst not eat them because they disagreed with his stomach'. On the morning of his death, Mr Delmis ate 'three buttered muffins for breakfast, before shooting himself, knowing that he should not be troubled with indigestion' (*Life* iii. 384). Boswell concludes his anecdote by mentioning that George Steevens stayed behind with Johnson and Beauclerk after their quarrel was patched up. The cancellans substitutes 'another gentleman' for Steevens's name and supplies dashes for the identities of the other two.

Though external pressure appears to have played a part in the cancellation of the 'conjugal infidelity' leaf, it was Boswell's concern for what might 'hurt the Book much' that proved decisive.

---

[64] Ibid. 401.

The biographer also took the initiative in the cancel we have just considered. The cancellation of four other leaves, by contrast, took place under duress—duress ranging from mild to severe. When Boswell's friend and dedicatee Joshua Reynolds changed his mind, and decided that he did not want the world to know of Johnson's contribution to his *Discourses on Art*, Boswell obliged by rewriting the passage in question. At the same time, he did Thomas Percy a favour by removing a comparable mention of Percy's indebtedness to Johnson (Fig. 4). However, the effect of this gesture was undermined by a telltale index entry. Although Percy suspected Boswell of duplicity, Malone convincingly exonerated him: 'The fact is, that the page in his book to which the Index refers is, a cancelled page; to which a reference was made by one Tomlins (who made the Index) when it was in its *original state*, before it was cancelled. . . . After the cancel was made, the Index was unluckily forgot to be changed or cancelled.'[65] In the cancellans, Boswell betrays a certain irritation at the anxiety of Reynolds and Percy to keep Johnson's assistance a secret: 'Some of these [contributions], the persons who were favoured with them are unwilling should be mentioned, from a too anxious apprehension, as I think, that they might be suspected of having received larger assistance' (*Life* ii. 2).

'Anxious apprehension' is too mild a term to describe the fervour with which Percy prosecuted his campaign for an additional cancel. Writing to Boswell on 24 March 1791, he took severe exception to a passage in which Johnson mocked the poet James Grainger's literary abilities and described Grainger as 'destitute of principle'.[66] Grainger, a close friend of Percy, had introduced him to Johnson; after Grainger's death, Percy

---

[65] *The Correspondence of Thomas Percy and Edmond Malone*, ed. Arthur Tillotson (New Haven: Yale Univ. Press, 1944), 56–7 (5 June 1792).

[66] Waingrow, 306–7; *Life MS* ii. 199–200.

defended his reputation from attacks in the press.[67] This campaign continued as the *Life* neared publication: after reading the conversation about Grainger in proof, Percy exhorted Boswell to remove Johnson's negative comments, on the grounds that to include them in the biography would prove 'as injurious to the Memory of the Relater, as to the Sufferer'. Percy went on to 'intreat' Boswell to 'cancel any accidental Escapes of the same kind where Dr. J. has thrown out Severe Censures on the personal Characters of Individuals'.[68] Though he was neither able nor willing to respond to Percy's more sweeping injunction, Boswell did censor the derogatory remarks about Grainger. However, in preparing the second edition he restored almost all the cancelled material, thereby ending his friendship with Percy.

Boswell's difficulties with importunate readers of his proof sheets—readers who misunderstood or even feared his devotion to authentic reportage—did not end with Percy. The minor politician William Gerard Hamilton objected, 'from the anxiety of [his] vanity', to being identified as the source of two seemingly innocuous anecdotes.[69] In another exasperated bulletin to Malone, Boswell reports, 'I shall have more cancels. That *nervous* mortal W[illiam] G[erard] H[amilton] is not satisfied with my report of some particulars *which I wrote down from his own mouth*, and is so much agitated, that Courtenay has persuaded me to allow a *new edition* of them by H. himself to be made at H.'s expence.'[70] Ultimately Boswell negotiated an agreement whereby Hamilton's name was removed, but Hamilton footed the

---

[67] Bertram H. Davis, *Thomas Percy: A Scholar-Cleric in the Age of Johnson* (Philadelphia: Univ. of Pennsylvania Press, 1989), 38, 206.

[68] Waingrow, 306–7.

[69] *Great Biographer*, 133 (3 Mar. 1791).

[70] Baker, 405–6 and n. 12.

substantial bill for the two cancels. Furthermore, Boswell took the occasion of the first cancel (Zz1) to add a sentence: '[Johnson] said to the Reverend Mr. Strahan, "Warburton is perhaps the last man who has written with a mind full of reading and reflection." '[71] Having been robbed of the kind of precise authenticating detail that he so much valued, Boswell was able to slip in, at the very last moment and at Hamilton's expense, an additional Johnsonian dictum. Almost until the official date of publication, 16 May 1791, the twin acts of imprinting galvanized each other.

It is time to step back from the tesserae we have been piecing together and consider the mosaic as a whole. How can we assess the design of the *Life* as it emerged out of two workshops, Boswell's and Baldwin's? The final *product* is a masterpiece, and masterpieces are always anomalous. But how unusual was the *process*? As we continue to explore the relationship between product and process, what compass points might help to orient us and to place individual discoveries within larger interpretative contexts? As a way of looking both backward and forward, I offer three preliminary conclusions.

First, the text of the first edition was affected to an unusual degree by the circumstances of production. Consider the state of the copy—one thousand leaves of densely revised manuscript doubled in size by the addition of complex Papers Apart. This copy, moreover, was in a state of flux throughout the fifteen months of printing. In addition, normal proofing procedures were suspended: the corrector could not make use of a reading boy and he depended for collating purposes on first proofs that were themselves ingenious *interpretations* of the copy. Nor did the author or the author's adviser collate on a regular basis. Finally, both compositor and corrector had the talent, the opportunity,

---

[71] *Life* iv. 49.

and the need to intervene creatively in the production of the text.

Second, Boswell—like Proust and Joyce in this respect—treated proofs almost as drafts. Consequently, as the *Life* moves through the press it evolves as much as it solidifies. Journal, manuscript, proofs, cancels, first edition, second edition, preparations for a third edition: at every stage Boswell seized the opportunity to polish and supplement his biographical *Odyssey*. *A la recherche* and *Ulysses*: to these we might add a third fictional analogue, *Tristram Shandy*. In the next chapter, I will be pointing toward affinities between Sterne's narrative games and Boswell's handling of space and time. Here I want to suggest a formal parallel between these two revolutionary works: both are simultaneously open and closed, fluid and fixed, finished and unfinished. Just as Sterne, had he lived, might well have continued his novel indefinitely, so Boswell might have gone on revising his biography. Both authors are cut down *in medias res*.

Third, the first edition of the *Life* offers a fascinating test case for revisionist theories of textual editing and bibliographic analysis, particularly those of Jerome J. McGann and D. F. McKenzie. In his *Critique of Modern Textual Criticism*, McGann makes a case for 'the social construction of meaning in a work and the necessity for considering the author or composer's intention as only one part of a continual collaborative process'.[72] McGann rejects what he considers Romantic concepts of textual autonomy and the editorial methods derived from them. In his view, the author is never autonomous, the work necessarily influenced by a set of complex historical circumstances. McGann reaches the conclusion that ' "final authority" for literary works rests neither with the author nor with his affiliated institution; it

---

[72] D. C. Greetham, 'Preface' to McGann, *A Critique of Modern Textual Criticism* (Charlottesville: Univ. of Virginia Press, 1992), p. xii.

resides in the actual structure of the agreements which these two cooperating authorities reach in specific cases'.[73]

Though McGann himself does not make the link, his critique correlates in certain respects with that of D. F. McKenzie. In 'Printers of the Mind' and other essays, McKenzie argues powerfully for an expanded concept of the text and for bibliographical work that combines deductive and inductive reasoning with an awareness of history and sociology. For McKenzie, 'bibliography should serve literature or the criticism of literature'; 'it may be thought to do this best, not by disappearing into its own minutiae, but by pursuing the study of printing history to the point where analysis can usefully begin.'[74] The issues raised by both McKenzie and McGann bring to the fore key questions about Boswell's *magnum opus*. How can analysis of the work as a literary artefact be enriched rather than diluted by 'the study of printing history'? If we approach the *Life* as the result of 'a continual collaborative process', is our assessment of Boswell's achievement enhanced or diminished? What does the making of this particular biography have to teach us about the genre as a whole—specifically, its complex mediation between the Aristotelian domains of poetry and history? These are questions I hope you will keep in mind as we continue to trace out Boswell's designs for, in, and upon the *Life of Johnson*.

[73] McGann, *Critique*, 54.

[74] McKenzie, 'Printers of the Mind: Some Notes on Bibliographical Theories and Printing-House Practices', *Studies in Bibliography*, 22 (1969), 61.

2

Representing Johnson

'The Flemish picture which I give of my friend': Boswell's metaphor both tantalizes and eludes. Its basic meaning is clear: the biographer conceives of his enterprise as analogous to that of a documentary portrait-painter who captures each 'small characteristick trait' of his subject (*Life* iii. 191). Like a Teniers or a Jordaens, Boswell commits himself to rendering unvarnished surfaces as a means of suggesting inspirational depths. Accordingly, he invites us to interpret his metaphor (and the method implicit in it) as a product of his most basic conviction: to see Johnson 'as he really was' (*Life* i. 30) is to admire and reverence him (*Life* iv. 430). The biographer's success, therefore, depends upon the arts of 'display' (*Life* i. 31).

To excavate the compositional layers of the *Life* is to apprehend, with a new clarity and conviction, Boswell's intuitive mastery of such arts. From first leaf to last, the manuscript allows us to reconstruct Boswell's picture-making tactics. For example, the revisions to the introductory statement of purpose show how carefully Boswell worked to present Johnson as a model in both senses of the term—'sitter' and 'guide'. The first version of this statement centres on the verb 'delineate': 'To be as he was is indeed subject of panegyrick enough to any man in this state of being, and when I delineate him without reserve, I do what he himself recommended both by his precept and his example.' But 'delineate' is not graphic enough; accordingly, Boswell heightens the portrait metaphor and connects the visual to the didactic by inserting a clause in mid-sentence. The final version reads: 'To be as he was is indeed subject of panegyrick enough to any man in this state of being, but in every picture there should be shade as well as light, and when I delineate him without reserve, I do what he himself recommended both by his precept and his example' (*Life MS* i. 11). To the medium of the sketch are added the chiaroscuro effects of an etching or an oil portrait.

At first glance, the metaphor of 'the Flemish picture' directs us toward Boswell's mimetic end and his means toward that end— the unsparing registration of characteristic and characterizing detail. As is often the case, however, when Boswell steps back to describe his methods, the comparison tells us little about the structural implications of the *concetto*. Therefore it is to the manuscript that we must turn in order to grasp the full significance of 'picture'. What such evidence helps us to understand, moreover, is that Boswell was creating a revolutionary paradigm for biography out of an ancient sister-arts tradition.[1] The nature of his innovation, as well as his debt to tradition, can best be understood through the lens of twentieth-century sister-arts criticism. Two concepts are of key importance: 'spatial form' and 'transactional biography'.

It was the signal achievement of Joseph Frank's 'Spatial Form in Modern Literature' to complicate Lessing's celebrated distinction between poetry and painting by locating in such twentieth-century works as Eliot's *Waste Land* and Barnes's *Nightwood* an attempt 'to overcome the time elements involved in their structures'.[2] According to Frank, a distinctive characteristic of literary modernism is the 'spatial interweaving of images

---

[1] For a concise and authoritative account of this tradition, see Rennselaer W. Lee, *Ut Pictura Poesis: The Humanistic Theory of Painting* (New York: Norton, 1967).

[2] Frank's essay appeared originally in the *Sewanee Review*, 53 (1945); it was reprinted in revised form in *The Widening Gyre* (New Brunswick, NJ: Rutgers Univ. Press, 1963). I quote from the essay as it appears in Frank's *The Idea of Spatial Form*—an indispensable volume that reviews the original essay and responds to critics (New Brunswick, NJ: Rutgers Univ. Press, 1991), 61.

and phrases', the experiment with a textual pattern that will suspend or dislocate chronological narrative. Over the half-century since its original publication, Frank's essay has provoked scores of responses;[3] the most important of these for our purposes is W. J. T. Mitchell's 'Spatial Form in Literature: Toward a General Theory'.[4] Mitchell extends and revises Frank's argument, moving in the process toward what he describes as 'a general theory of literary space'. Such a theory, Mitchell contends, would be grounded in the claim that every literary text is a spatial form, and that every reading experience has the capacity either to suspend us in 'an eternally timeless realm' or to 'produce the illusion of temporal sequence'. Therefore, 'instead of viewing space and time as antithetical modalities, we ought to treat their relationship as one of complex interaction, interdependence, and interpenetration'.[5]

Both Frank and Mitchell point to *Tristram Shandy* as a sophisticated example of spatial form in fictional narrative. Its contemporary non-fictional counterpart, I would argue, is the *Life of Johnson*, a textual mosaic that embodies a 'complex interaction' between space and time. Just as the biography's multiple conversations contribute to the portrait of the protagonist, so Boswell's 'Flemish picture' participates in (and is modified by) the temporal arc of the *Life*. Though seemingly at odds with each other, static and kinetic elements collaborate to create the very experience that Boswell celebrates at the outset:

Indeed I cannot conceive a more perfect mode of writing any man's life, than not only relating all the most important events of it in their

[3] See in particular Frank's charting of critical reaction in *The Idea of Spatial Form*, as well as *Spatial Form in Narrative*, ed. Jeffrey R. Smitten and Ann Daghistany (Ithaca, NY: Cornell Univ. Press, 1981).

[4] Mitchell (ed.), *The Language of Images* (Chicago: Univ. of Chicago Press, 1980), 271–99.   [5] Ibid. 276.

order, but interweaving what he privately wrote, and said, and thought; by which mankind are enabled as it were to see him live, and to 'live o'er each scene' with him, as he actually advanced through the several stages of his life. (*Life* i. 30)

This declaration, like the work it introduces, finely balances the activities of 'living' and 'seeing', 'relating' in time and 'interweaving' in space. As theatrical constructs, moreover, the 'scenes' of the *Life* tell stories and make pictures simultaneously. It is for these reasons that the concept of spatial form helps us to elucidate the 'interweaving' of materials and to analyse the impact of the patterns that result.

The same concept can only take us so far, however, when we attempt to grasp the composition, the placement, and the total effect of those multiple portraits that form the biography's image of Johnson. The essential make-up of this composite image will come more sharply into focus if we turn to *Sir Joshua Reynolds: The Painter in Society*, Richard Wendorf's recent study of the biography's dedicatee. In elucidating Reynolds's complex *œuvre*, Wendorf makes effective use of what he calls 'a transactional theory of portraiture'. According to Wendorf, 'such a theory . . . challenges much traditional thinking about portraiture by drawing particular attention to the complicated dynamics of the studio and the sitting: to the importance, that is, of the environment and process out of which the finished canvas emerges'.[6] As the term 'transactional' suggests, the approach invites us to consider a portrait as the record of a series of encounters between subject and artist. It thereby emphasizes the collaborative and

---

[6] Wendorf, *Sir Joshua Reynolds: The Painter in Society* (Cambridge, Mass.: Harvard Univ. Press, 1996), 4. Though he does not use the term 'transactional portraiture', Richard Brilliant makes a similar point when he observes that 'the act of portrayal involves the portraitist in the formation of his ostensible subject . . . [G]reat portraits express that social relationship as part of their primary meaning' (Brilliant, *Portraiture* (Cambridge, Mass.: Harvard Univ. Press, 1991), 128).

performative process out of which the likeness emerges. Reading a portrait is tantamount to investigating 'the relationship between artist and sitter' and interpreting the image as the result of a dynamic exchange.

To approach the *Life* from this perspective is to view afresh the importance of three transactions. The first and most basic is that between biographer and subject. By 1773, Johnson knew that Boswell intended to write his life, and in the journal of their Hebridean tour he sampled its preliminary version. The terms of his praise both adumbrate and validate Boswell's 'Flemish' method: 'I am most scrupulously exact in this Journal. Mr. Johnson said it was a very exact picture of his life.'[7] The second transaction is that between Boswell and Edmond Malone, whose close encounters we have charted in Chapter 1. The transaction most relevant to the topic of biographical portraiture is the dynamic relationship between Boswell and Sir Joshua Reynolds. This relationship, which influenced every stage of Boswell's project, might even have yielded another masterpiece: within months of the publication of the *Life of Johnson*, Boswell was collecting notes for a life of Reynolds.[8] What form *that* biography would have taken is a question that haunts this enquiry.

Boswell's debts to Reynolds begin early and take various forms. Five years before he had decided 'to write Dr. Johnson's life in scenes',[9] Boswell was conceiving of his project in pictorial terms, and connecting it with the painter's procedures. The

---

[7] *Boswell's Journal of* A Tour to the Hebrides, ed. Frederick A. Pottle and Charles Bennett (New York: Viking, 1936), 245 (3 Oct. 1773). For a thorough and thought-provoking discussion of the topic, see John B. Radner, '"A Very Exact Picture of his Life": Johnson's Role in Writing the *Life of Johnson*', *Age of Johnson*, 7 (1996), 299–342.

[8] *Literary Career*, 308.

[9] *Boswell, Laird of Auchinleck 1778–1782*, ed. Joseph W. Reed and Frederick A. Pottle (New York: McGraw-Hill, 1977), 260 (12 Oct. 1780).

earliest fully articulated conception of biography as portraiture occurs in the journal entry for 27 March 1775:

I half persuaded him to go with me to Beauclerk's. But he suddenly took a resolution to go home, saying, 'But I don't love Beauclerk the less'; or something quite to that effect, for I am so nice in recording him that every trifle must be authentic. I draw him in the style of a Flemish painter. I am not satisfied with hitting the large features. I must be exact as to every hair, or even every spot on his countenance.[10]

The context is highly suggestive: earlier that same day, Boswell had accompanied Johnson to Sir Joshua's house and studio, where Frances Reynolds was painting Johnson's portrait. As Johnson sat to Frances, Boswell read 'some passages' from his Hebridean journal to her brother, who was warm in its praise. Ten years later, Boswell commissioned a portrait of himself from Reynolds four days after beginning to revise the *Tour* for publication; sessions with Reynolds and sessions with Malone proceeded in tandem throughout the summer of 1785, and portrait and book were finished within two days of each other.[11] It is during this period that Boswell added to his original journal a 'Character' of Johnson that 'serve[s] to introduce to the fancy of [his] readers the capital object of the following journal'. This Character takes the form of 'an imperfect sketch of "the *combination* and the *form*" of that Wonderful Man'.[12] The quotation from *Hamlet* comes from the closet scene, in which Gertrude is forced to compare the portraits of her first and second husbands:

---

[10] *Boswell: The Ominous Years 1774–1776*, ed. Charles Ryskamp and Frederick A. Pottle (New York: McGraw-Hill, 1963), 103 (27 Mar. 1775).

[11] *Boswell: The Applause of the Jury 1782–1785*, ed. Irma S. Lustig and Frederick A. Pottle (New York: McGraw-Hill, 1981), 306, 308–9, 317, 340.

[12] *Tour to the Hebrides*, ed. Pottle and Bennett, 9. To avoid confusion, I will continue to capitalize 'character' when the word designates Boswell's psycho-physical epitome of Johnson.

Look here upon this picture, and on this,
The counterfeit presentment of two brothers.
See what a grace was seated on this brow. . .
A combination and a form indeed
Where every god did seem to set his seal
To give the world assurance of a man.[13]

As with the earlier comparison of biography and portrait-painting, Boswell writes out of direct experience: for the second time, a portrait-in-the-making influences a portrait-in-the-making.

Within a year or two of Boswell's preliminary exercise in biographical portraiture, Sir Joshua composed his own 'sketch'—a brief memoir that F. W. Hilles aptly calls 'a word-portrait'.[14] In the framing passages of the *Life*—the dedication to Reynolds and the concluding Character—Boswell made significant use of this memoir, absorbing not only its contents but also its figurative language. Indeed the pictorial metaphor first appears in a passage that dialogues silently as well as explicitly with Reynolds: 'You, my dear Sir, studied him, and knew him well: you venerated and admired him. Yet, luminous as he was upon the whole, you perceived all the shades which mingled in the grand composition; all the little peculiarities and slight blemishes which marked the literary Colossus' (*Life* i. 2). But Boswell's debt does not stop there. His opening drumroll—which combines the mock humility topos with the confident assertion of an authority based on intimate friendship—derives from Reynolds's introduction as well. The painter gives the biographer carte blanche:

From thirty years' intimacy with Dr. Johnson I certainly have had the means, if I had equally the ability, of giving you a true and perfect idea

---

[13] *William Shakespeare: Collected Works*, ed. Alfred Harbage (Baltimore: Penguin, 1969), 957 (III. iv. 54–6, 61–3).

[14] Frederick W. Hilles (ed.), *Portraits by Sir Joshua Reynolds*, (New York: McGraw-Hill, 1952), 71.

of the character and peculiarities of this extraordinary man. The habits of my profession unluckily extend to the consideration of so much only of character as lies on the surface, as is expressed in the lineaments of the countenance. An attempt to go deeper and investigate the peculiar colouring of his mind, as distinguished from all other minds, nothing but your earnest desire can excuse the presumption even of attempting. Such as it is, you may make what use of it you please.[15]

And Boswell did exactly that, appropriating models and materials from Sir Joshua in both his roles—practioner of the sister art of portrait-painting and a privileged biographical source who refuses to deal in 'panegyric'.[16]

The example of Reynolds also motivates and supports the rhythmical restatement of the portrait metaphor throughout the biography. Early in his narrative for 1764, Boswell inserts a Paper Apart (designated 'O', presumably for 'Oddity') that describes 'the most minute singularities which belonged to him and made very observable parts of his appearance and manner' (*Life MS* i. 340). Boswell resisted Malone's attempt to relegate most of the description to a note, and turned to Reynolds for supporting testimony: 'Sir Joshua Reynolds has known him to go a good way about rather than cross [an>] a particular alley in Liecester=fields; but this Sir Joshua imputed to his having had some disagreable recollection associated with it' (*Life MS* i.340). This Paper Apart ends with a justification that echoes the dedicatory tribute to Reynolds: 'Now I am fully aware how very obvious an occasion I here give for the sneering jocularity of such as have no relish of an exact likeness, which to render complete

   [15] Hilles (ed.), *Portraits*, 74.

   [16] 'You will wonder to hear a person who loved him so sincerely speak thus freely of his friend, but you must recollect I am not writing his panegyric' (ibid. 82). This declaration underlies Boswell's: 'And he will be seen as he really was; for I profess to write, not his Panegyrick, which must be all praise, but his Life' (*Life MS* i. 10).

he who draws it must not disdain the slightest strokes' (*Life MS* i. 340) Similarly Boswell affiliates himself with Reynolds when it comes time, within the narrative for 1773, to take stock of the *Journal of a Tour to the Hebrides*. The passage that describes his achievement is reworked to emphasize the picture-making powers of the *Tour*:

[The force and>] His various adventures and the force and vivacity of his mind, as exercised during this Peregrination upon innumerable topicks [had been faithfully recorded by me>] have been faithfully and to the best of my abilities displayed in my 'Journal of a Tour to the Hebrides' to which as the Publick has been pleased to honour it by a very extensive circulation I beg leave to refer, as to a separate and remarkable [period/part/portion] portion of his Life which may be there [viewed>] seen in detail and which exhibits as striking [a view of his mind/a specimen of his powers>] a view of his powers in conversation as his works do of his excellence in writing. (*Life MS* ii. 118)

Boswell then instructs the compositor to insert fourteen lines from John Courtenay's *Poetical Review of the Literary and Moral Character of Dr. Johnson*. Boswell and Malone were virtual co-authors of this poem, so that the lines in question can be interpreted as something close to self-encomium.[17] The verse paragraph begins by inviting us to imagine the page as a canvas:

> With Reynolds' pencil, vivid, bold, and true,
> So fervent Boswell gives him to our view.
> In every trait we see his mind expand;
> The master rises by the pupil's hand.[18]

These references to 'viewing' and 'seeing' echo and reinforce Boswell's unmediated descriptions of his enterprise; moreover, they link his procedures as closely as possible to Reynolds's.

---

[17] For Boswell's part in the making of Courtenay's *Poetical Review*, see Baker, 287–8, 301–2.

[18] Quoted in ibid. 288 n. 8.

The journal entry that resulted from a visit to Reynolds's studio ('I draw him in the style of a Flemish painter') generates a passage in the *Life* manuscript that intensifies Boswell's commitment to visual specificity: 'But I draw the portrait of Johnson in the style of a flemish painter. I am not satisfied with hitting the large features. I must be exact as to every line in his countenance every hair, every mole' (ii. 139). The paragraph in which this passage occurs is deleted—an abbreviated version of it resurfacing under 1777, where it glosses a narrative derived from Boswell's Ashbourne journal: 'This may be laughed at as too trifling to record; but it is a small characteristick trait in the Flemish picture which I give of my friend, and in which, therefore, I mark the most minute particulars' (*Life* iii. 191). The evidence of the manuscript suggests that this deletion occurred after Boswell had added a paragraph on mimicry. The paragraph begins: 'I have been considered by those who knew Johnson best as being able to imitate most exactly his manner in all respects' (*Life MS* ii. 140). The underlying metaphor here is musical, not visual, but the language suggests that Boswell thought of the two enterprises— 'Flemish' portraiture, accurate mimicry—as interrelated. For example, Boswell's first impulse was to describe an actor who specialized in imitations of Johnson as 'a good mimick of some persons [but one who] did not hit the likeness of Johnson' (*Life MS* ii. 140–1). In proof Malone altered 'hit the likeness of Johnson' to 'represent Johnson correctly'—thereby obscuring what Boswell perceived as the connection between pointillist technique in verbal portraiture and the art of capturing every intonation of His Master's Voice.

At one remarkable moment, Johnson the sitter becomes Johnson the portraitist, joining Boswell and Reynolds in the wielding of a biographical 'pencil'. On 5 April 1776, Boswell reports, he 'gave us one of the many sketches of character which were treasured in his mind, and which he was wont to produce quite unexpectedly in a very entertaining manner' (MS 562). Boswell turns the resulting 'sketch' into evidence of Johnson's discernment of character and his descriptive powers:

It was a very remarkable circumstance about Johnson (who was reckoned ignorant of the World) that very few men had seen greater variety of characters, and none could observe them better, as was evident from the strong yet nice portraits which he drew of them. [I have often thought that if he had made out what the french call a Catalogue raisonnee of all the people with whom he was acquainted it would have been a very rich fund of information>] I have often thought that if he had made out what the french call une Catalogue raisonnee of all the people who had passed under his observation it would have afforded a very rich fund of instruction and entertainment. (MS 563–4)[19]

The Johnson who draws 'strong yet nice portraits' of his acquaintance is a figure ideally suited to the 'strong yet nice' portrait drawn of him. And Johnson the potential author of a *catalogue raisonné* implicitly validates Boswell's own visual stocktaking, which supplements pictorial metaphors with a succession of verbal portraits. Indeed the concept of the *Life* as a giant exhibition catalogue appears to have influenced the expansion of the title, which starts out in trial proof as curtly and colourlessly as possible: '*The Life of Samuel Johnson, LL.D.*' (Fig. 5). The version that emerges from final proof is comprehensive in scope and pictorial in language; it cues us, like the beginning of Pope's *Epistle to a Lady*, to stroll the length of a portrait-gallery: *The Life of Samuel Johnson, LL.D. comprehending An Account of his Studies and Numerous Works, in Chronological Order, A Series of his Epistolary Correspondence and Conversations with Many Eminent Persons; Also, Various Original Pieces of his Composition, the Whole Exhibiting a View of Literature and Literary Men in Great-Britain, For Near Half a Century, During Which*

[19] MSS 562–4: Houghton Library, Harvard University.

He Flourished. Johnson's 'original pieces', the punning title suggests, compose Boswell's panoramic conversation-piece.

Precedents and paradigms for such a gallery are provided by the 'sketch' in the *Tour* and by Reynolds's 'word-portrait'. In addition, two revealing passages (one from the memoranda and the other from the manuscript itself) make explicit the aesthetic warrant for Boswell's use of verbal cameos. The memorandum registers his concern with activating the reader's visual imagination from the outset: 'His person and manner should be painted early so as he may be seen as his life advances' (M157; *Life MS* i. 64 n. 3). In a manuscript passage that Boswell subsequently deleted, he elaborates the conceit of biographical portraiture:

[And it will be considered by the judicious and the candid judges of biography that such little particulars afford/give the justest and most lively representation of a character. They are like those small delicate touches of the hand of a masterly Painter by which a portrait is vivified/quickened, and the light of animation is thrown upon the larger parts/whole component of the countenance *del*] (*Life MS* i. 275–6)

'Small delicate touches of the hand of a masterly Painter': as the biography proceeds, these 'touches' both constitute and imply the 'whole component of the countenance'.

Just as Reynolds painted multiple portraits of Johnson, which track him through three decades, so Boswell provides multiple takes on his sitter. Three descriptive passages are of special importance, for they help to image Johnson's 'person and manner' during the early phases of the biography. Each passage contains a cameo portrait, which 'gives him to our view' and thereby animates what amounts to a conversion experience: Johnson meets the individual in question, who is shocked by his appearance but then won over by his extraordinary intellect and eloquence. A sense of Johnson's fleshly presence, of his visual specificity and peculiarity, is crucial to the emotional and intellectual curve of these encounters. In order to 'live o'er each scene' from the point of view of the convert, the reader/viewer must experience first the shock of repulsion and then the tug of attraction. Boswell selects his 'touches' with great care, and the result is precisely to 'quicken' the narrative. Here too the manuscript furnishes new evidence, new pentimenti.

Boswell's account of the initial encounter between Johnson and Elizabeth Porter allows us to see him through her eyes, and to experience the metamorphosis of freak into lover:

> Miss Porter told me that when he was first introduced to her Mother, his appearance was [shocking/very forbidding>] very forbidding. He was then lean and lank, so that his immense structure of bones was hideously striking to the eye, and the scars of the scrophula were deeply visible. He also wore his hair, which was straight and stiff, and separated behind ∧and he often had seemingly convulsive starts and odd gesticulations which tended to excite at once surprise and ridicule∧. But [her mother>] Mrs. Porter was so much engaged by his conversation that she overlooked all these external disadvantages, and said ∧to her daughter∧ 'this is the most sensible man that I ever saw in my life.' (*Life MS* i. 64)

The choice of 'forbidding' over 'shocking' is significant: it prepares for the physical data that follow, but it also interprets these data as a barrier, thereby injecting a note of agreeable uncertainty—will the great divide be crossed? Boswell attends to 'the larger parts': with refined economy of means, he creates a sense of mass, of the body in space. At the same time, he supplies minute particulars (the scars, the hair, the gesticulations) that imply an entire physical and emotional history. We feel, as Mrs Porter must have felt, a mixture of pity and distaste. This well-focused display of Johnson's 'external disadvantages' helps to index the extent of his compensatory powers. Moreover, the force of 'but' derives principally from the miniature portrait that precedes it.

A similar strategy underlies Boswell's presentation of the first meeting between Johnson and Bennet Langton. In this case, however, the initial shock is more intense, for Langton had painted his own imaginary portrait of the writer whose works he so much admired. Langton's pre-existing image must be drastically revised, and Boswell recreates the process of adjustment by supplying a vivid counter-portrait:

From perusing his Writings he fancied he should see a [decent/decorous well=drest well=bred] decent well=drest in short a remarkably decorous Philosopher. Instead of which, down from his bed=chamber [about noon came as just risen/just risen about noon came>] about noon came as newly risen [a person with all the extraordinary circumstances which I have mentioned as united in Johnson>] a huge uncouth figure with a little dark wig which scarcely covered his head, and his clothes hanging loose about him. But his conversation was so rich so animated and so forcible, and his [religious and political notions/ notions of religion & government>] religious and political notions so congenial with those in which Mr. Langton had been educated, that he conceived for him that veneration and attachment which he ever preserved. (*Life MS* i. 177)

The successive revisions make it clear that Boswell's first impulse is to refer the reader to previous descriptions: 'a person with all the extraordinary circumstances which I have mentioned as united in Johnson.' But he then decides to 'vivify' the scene with 'delicate little touches'—in this instance, the startling contrast between 'huge uncouth figure' and 'little dark wig', not to mention the indecorous dishabille. As in the previous cameo, the 'but' registers with such force because of the image that has been conjured up for us—an image that is both indelible (for we can never forget those details) and inconsequential (for conversation trumps appearance).

The third cameo and the third conversion experience occur when Boswell first calls upon Johnson at his chambers:

He received me very courteously; but, it must be confessed that [the appearance of the apartment and furniture and his morning dress were by no means/ the reverse of being elegant or neat>] his apartment and furniture and morning dress were sufficiently uncouth. [A very characteristical Anecdote/circumstance has been told by an ingenious gentleman how one day Johnson called out 'A clean chair for Mrs. Cholmondeley' upon being surprised with a visit from that Lady. *del*] His brown suit of clothes looked very [rusty/dirty/old>] rusty; he had [a little old shrivelled unpowdered wig upon the top of his head,>] on a little old shrivelled unpowdered wig which was too small for his head, his shirt neck and knees of his breeches were loose ˄his black worsted stockings ill drawn up˄ and he had a pair of unbuckled shoes by way of slippers. But all these slovenly particularities were forgotten, [the moment that he/when he>] the moment that he began to talk. (*Life MS* i. 273)

Once again the manuscript testifies to Boswell's search for the significant detail, his care for verbal portraiture. In revising he settles upon a word ('uncouth') that perfectly captures Johnson's milieu and manner. Because he wishes to concentrate on a figure in the landscape, he deletes the anecdote that intervenes between description of setting and appearance of protagonist (the anecdote does not resurface elsewhere, and therefore we will never know the outcome of Mrs Cholmondeley's visit). He settles on an adjective, 'rusty', that suggests both colour and texture. He reworks the description of Johnson's headpiece so as to emphasize the discrepancy in size ('a little old shrivelled unpowdered wig which was too small for his head') and he adds the detail of the stockings. At this, his second encounter with Johnson, Boswell supplies a portrait of the sage *en pantoufles*.

Connected to these three episodes is a potential conversion experience, which asks us to visualize Johnson under circumstances that make it impossible for powers of mind and rhetoric to overcome external disadvantages. The consequence is a 'but', a triumphant reversal, that never happens. In a hypothetical parliamentary setting, Boswell positions a version of the 'uncouth' Johnson he has been etching so indelibly:

It has been much agitated among his friends and others whether [there was good reason to expect that *del*] he would have been a powerful speaker in Parliament had he been brought in when advanced in life. [I should have supposed that his ready force of mind his strength and richness of expression his wit and humour and above all his sarcastical keeness might have had great effect in a popular assembly; and that the bulkiness of his figure and striking peculiarity of his manner would have aided the effect/impression>] I am inclined to think that his ˄extensive knowledge, his˄ quickness and force of mind his vivacity and richness of expression his wit and humour and above all his poignancy of sarcasm would have had great effect in a popular assembly; and that the magnitude of his figure and striking peculiarity of his manner would have aided the effect. (*Life MS* ii. 65)

The original version of this passage activates memories not only of the three cameos but also of the explanation for Johnson's fiasco as a teacher, which Boswell attributes in part to 'his oddities of manner and uncouth gesticulations' (*Life MS* i. 67). In so doing, it creates an imaginary scene, 'Johnson Addressing the House of Commons', that both laments and explains his failure by juxtaposing 'ready force of mind', 'strength and richness of expression', 'wit and humour', and 'sarcastical keeness' to 'bulkiness of . . . figure' and 'striking peculiarity of . . . manner'. The visual details, especially the word 'bulkiness', conjure up a picture so vivid that it undercuts Boswell's ostensible point: appearance would have assisted 'force of mind'. For this reason, perhaps, the revised passage blurs the evocation of Johnson's ungainly body and startling eccentricities by settling on Latinate periphrastic expressions ('vivacity' for 'strength', 'magnitude' for 'bulkiness', 'poignancy of sarcasm' for 'sarcastical keeness').

These four portraits, and others like them, act as verbal counterparts to, extensions of, and commentaries upon the frontispiece that introduced the eighteenth-century reader to the subject of the *Life*. Along with the dedication and the final Character, this frontispiece best exemplifies the transactional, collaborative dimension of Boswell's massive portrait. As he neared the end of the biography, Boswell employed James Heath to engrave Reynolds's first portrait of Johnson, which depicts him as the great lexicographer, quill in hand, with a volume of the *Dictionary* on the adjacent table (Fig. 6). This portrait, which Reynolds never finished, had stayed in his studio for over three decades. The layers of revision in the manuscript, combined with annotated copies of the engraving in its second and third states, allow us to reconstruct what happened as publication drew near (Figs. 8, 9).

Boswell had decided, in the account of his first meeting with Johnson, to delete the original descriptive passage: 'Mr. Johnson is a Man of a most dreadfull appearance. He is a very big Man, is troubled with sore eyes, the Palsy and the Kings evil. He is very slovenly in his dress and speaks with a most uncouth voice.' In place of these details, Boswell substituted a reference to the Reynolds portrait: 'I found that I had a very perfect idea of Johnson's figure from a picture of him by Sir Joshua Reynolds in the attitude of sitting in his easy-chair in deep meditation which was the first picture his friend did for him. It has never been finished, though I cannot but help thinking it a striking likeness.' Once Boswell had decided to reproduce this portrait as his frontispiece, he insisted that Heath alter the engraving under the direction of Sir Joshua himself: Johnson's 'countenance', the two men decided, was 'too young and not thoughtful enough'. Reynolds then finished the portrait so as to conform it to the engraving, and presented the picture to Boswell, who then brought his account up to date. The final layer of revision reads: 'I found that I had a very perfect idea of Johnson's figure, from a picture of him by Sir Joshua Reynolds in the attitude of sitting in his easy-chair in deep meditation, soon after he had published his Dictionary, which was the first picture his friend did for him, of which Sir Joshua has been so very good as to make me a present and from which an engraving has been made for this work' (*Life MS* i. 269).

At least three factors help to explain the decision to impart visual information by pictorial means. First, the physical details that bulk large in the original journal entry have already been conveyed to the reader, largely through the cameo portraits we have just been examining. Second, the reference to the frontispiece (which prompts the reader to turn back to the beginning of the book) reinforces the other markers of space and movement and thereby enhances the theatricality of the moment: we can recreate in our mind's eye not only the appearance of Tom Davies ('somewhat in the manner of an actor in the part of Horatio') but also of Johnson (cast as the Ghost of Hamlet's Father).[20] Third, the reference to the frontispiece enhances Boswell's authority and credibility by affiliating his enterprise with Reynolds. The engraving is inscribed, 'Samuel Johnson, From the original Picture in the Possession of James Boswell Esq.' This authorized icon presides over the biography as an image jointly constituted by painter-biographer and biographer-painter. It functions as an illustration of, correlative to, and warrant for Boswell's textual representation of his subject.[21]

---

[20] Richard Wendorf makes a similar point when he astutely observes, 'Because Reynolds's painting is more direct, more efficient, more immediate than a full-length portrait in prose, it works to keep the drama alive at this crucial point in the text' (Wendorf, *The Elements of Life: Biography and Portrait-Painting in Stuart and Georgian England* (Oxford: Clarendon Press, 1990), 289).

[21] See Irma S. Lustig, 'Facts and Deductions: The Curious History of Reynolds's First Portrait of Johnson, 1756', *Age of Johnson*, 1 (1987), 161–80; Kai Kin Yung, *Samuel Johnson 1709–1784* (London: Herbert Press, 1984), 79–83.

Framing the vast expanse of the *Life* are the frontispiece and the final Character, which was composed during the climactic burst of activity that also produced the dedication. It is telling that the biography's opening and closing pages should have emerged from the same compositional phase: the Character not only makes silent use of Reynolds's memoir;[22] it also aspires to match Reynolds's visual artistry with a verbal icon that will reincarnate Johnson at the end of the long journey.

Johnson disappears from sight some five months (and fifty pages) before he dies. Boswell shapes the account of their last face-to-face meeting so that its contours evoke the topography of their first significant farewell. In August 1763 the two men had 'parted with tenderness' on the beach at Harwich: 'As the vessel put out to sea, I kept my eyes upon him for a considerable time, while he remained rolling his majestick frame in his usual manner: and at last I perceived him walk back into the town, and he disappeared' (*Life* i. 472). In July 1784 Boswell and Johnson '[bid] adieu to each other affectionately' outside Bolt Court; and as Sir Joshua Reynolds's coach pulls away, Boswell watches from inside as Johnson '[springs] away with a kind of pathetick briskness . . . which seemed to indicate a struggle to conceal uneasiness, and impressed me with a foreboding of our long, long separation' (*Life* iv. 339).

After this scene, the last fully dramatized moment in the biography, our view of Johnson is obscured by a barrage of documentation. In effect, Boswell reverses the movement with which the biography began—a movement from archival collage into fully visual, fully theatrical incarnation. Even when his hero lies dying, he refuses to supply any kind of scene or tableau.[23] To

---

[22] See in particular Hilles (ed.), *Portraits*, 75.

[23] As Donald J. Newman observes, Boswell 'deliberately abandons the biographical method that has been his constant boast' (Newman, 'The Death Scene

our considerable frustration, an array of doctors' reports, legal documents, and eyewitness anecdotes holds us at arm's length. When Johnson expires, moreover, the event is handled with chronicle-like neutrality and brevity. 'As to the Death', Boswell tells Malone, 'I shall be concise though solemn'[24]—and so it proves:

Having, as has been already mentioned, made his will on the 8th and 9th of December, and settled all his worldly affairs, he languished till Monday, the 13th of that month, when he expired, about seven o'clock in the evening, with so little apparent pain that his attendants hardly perceived when his dissolution took place. (*Life* iv. 417)

So colourless and cryptic is the reportage that we too 'hardly perceive when his dissolution took place': dramatic immediacy is sacrificed to documentary authenticity. Although it may seem perverse, this is a deliberate decision, as Boswell informs the reader: 'it is not my intention to give a very minute detail of the particulars of Johnson's remaining days' (*Life* iv. 398–9).

Commentators have differed widely in their assessment of local manœuvres, but most of them conclude that the final phase of the *Life*, considered as a whole, must be judged deficient and even dishonest. The most inventive riposte to this critical consensus comes from Donna Heiland, who analyses the massive annotation that intrudes upon the narrative of Johnson's final months. For Heiland, 'what has been depicted in this whole series of footnotes is equivalent to the dissemination of Johnson's body. Cultural analogues for such a phenomenon include the Dionysian ritual of *sparagmos*—in which a sacrificial body often identified with the god is torn to pieces, and then consumed,

and the Art of Suspense in Boswell's *Life of Johnson*', in John A. Vance (ed.), *Boswell's* Life of Johnson: *New Questions, New Answers* (Athens: Univ. of Georgia Press, 1985), 54.

[24] Baker, 400.

in the separate ritual of *omophagia*—as well as the Christian counterpart to these two rituals, the celebration of the Eucharist.' Heiland expands upon this point by drawing attention to the interplay between the disrupted narrative and the disrupted page: 'Even as the *Life* images this fragmenting and scattering of Johnson's body, it at the same time represents and so repeats the process it describes. . . . By the end of the *Life*, one is reading about Johnson in discontinuous chunks.'[25]

Heiland's provocative parallels sharpen our awareness of Boswell's daring sense of an ending—specifically, his decision to abrogate the biographical contract by leaving us with 'chunks' or tesserae. This heap of fragments helps first to conceal and then to bury Johnson. It would seem that the biographer we had come to admire will now—out of striking misjudgement, sheer perversity, or puzzling failure of nerve—fob us off with a will, a monument, or someone else's 'sepulchral verses':

A monument for him, in Westminster-Abbey, was resolved upon. . . . and in the cathedral of his native city of Lichfield, a smaller one is to be erected. To compose his epitaph, could not but excite the warmest competition of genius. If *laudari a laudato viro* be praise which is highly estimable, I should not forgive myself were I to omit the following sepulchral verses on the author of THE ENGLISH DICTIONARY, written by the Right Honourable Henry Flood. (*Life* iv. 423–4)

Apres lui, le Déluge. But then, almost without warning, Johnson is back, in all his glorious complexity and specificity. The tactic is bold, surprising, and even shocking, for Johnson returns to us as Jesus reappears to his disciples on the road to Emmaus. Boswell brilliantly adapts the conclusion of Luke's Gospel, as filtered through the hagiographic tradition, to produce an epiphany that

---

[25] Heiland, 'Remembering the Hero in Boswell's *Life of Johnson*', in Greg Clingham (ed.), *New Light on Boswell* (Cambridge: Cambridge Univ. Press, 1991), 199–200.

depends upon the bodily manifestation of the dead hero. We are made to *see* Johnson with a fresh and final intensity. Though the encounter is elegiac, the apparition is far from spectral. The success of Boswell's daring endgame depends not only on the disappearing act that has preceded it but on the ability of the Character itself to offer a portrait that is familiar yet fresh, coherent yet complex. By measuring this portrait against its predecessor in the *Tour*, and by attending to the testimony of the manuscript, we can observe how scrupulously Boswell designed the final manifestation of Johnson.

In a letter to Malone, written as the end of the marathon approached, Boswell wonders whether he should 'give the Character in my Tour, somewhat enlarged'.[26] Malone's response is characteristic, for it admonishes Boswell to subordinate the eccentric to the edifying: 'With respect to the Character in your Journal, if you retain it, it certainly should be amplified, and his uniform piety and virtue enlarged upon.'[27] A footnote in the manuscript appears to indicate that Boswell did indeed take advantage of his earlier experiment in biographical portraiture: 'As I certainly do not see any reason to give a different character of my illustrious friend now from what I formerly did, the greatest part of the sketch of him in my Journal of A Tour to the Hebrides . . . is here adopted' (MS 1038). However, the suggestion that the Character at the end of the *Life* virtually duplicates that at the beginning of the *Tour* is more than a little misleading. The first and most obvious point to make is that Boswell's decision to conclude with the Character causes it to register in a much different way—as magisterial synthesis rather than introductory profile. Boswell takes special pains, in fact, to emphasize the Character as a definitive portrait, which will 'collect into one

---

[26] Baker, 400.
[27] Ibid. 408.

view the capital and distinguishing features of this extraordinary man'. This formulation has the further advantage of echoing and fulfilling the words of the title page, which has promised to '[exhibit] a View of Literature and Literary Men in Great-Britain'.

The second major difference between the two Characters is that the version in the *Tour*, despite being labelled a 'sketch', shows little care for compositional coherence and the relationship of outward appearance to inner reality. In fact, the most striking feature of this preliminary version is its relative neglect of visual data. Boswell attends first to Johnson's religious and political convictions, next to his intellectual and creative capacities. And when it comes, the first physical detail is non-visual: 'He had a loud voice and a slow deliberate utterance which no doubt gave some additional weight to the sterling metal of his conversation.'[28] Only then does Boswell furnish the information that helps us to visualize Johnson: 'His person was large, robust, I may say approaching to the gigantic, and grown unwieldy from corpulency. His countenance was naturally of the cast of an ancient statue, but somewhat disfigured by the scars of that *evil* which it was formerly imagined the *royal touch* could cure.'[29] The *Tour* takes us from depth to surface, the *Life* from surface to depth. One consequence of this reversal is the assimilation of the corporeal to the intellectual. We are compelled to read the inner through the outer man—and ultimately to fuse the two. The result, unprecedented and unforgettable, is a fully reincarnated Johnson.

This startling achievement, however, is not won without fundamental rethinking and revision. Like its predecessor in the *Tour*, the Character in the *Life* starts out by downplaying

[28] *Tour to the Hebrides*, ed. Pottle and Bennett, 7.
[29] Ibid. 8.

the pictorial. We approach details of appearance ('His figure was large and well formed . . .') through a series of rather colourless generalizations about human nature; these, combined with statements about Johnson's temperament and conduct, tend to diffuse the impact of descriptive detail. Censorious remarks on 'prejudices unworthy of a great mind' do even more to interrupt the picture-making distillation.[30] But when he undertakes a structural overhaul of the Character, Boswell vigorously prunes his intrusive commentary—remembering to 'exhibit' his sitter and thereby keeping the promise he had made as the *Life* entered its final stages ('I now relieve the readers of this Work from any farther personal notice of its authour'). At the same time, Boswell repositions the *sententiae*, pushes visual details to the fore, and 'reads' his portrait in the act of painting it.

'With how small a speck does a painter give life to an eye!'[31] Boswell animates his subject for one last time by modifying brush strokes as well as repainting entire sections. These small but significant adjustments continue right through the stage of revised proof. Though they take various forms, they work toward the same end: the presentation and intensification of the Character as icon.

Boswell begins to alert the reader and to create an interpretative context for the Character by tallying up the existing portraits of Johnson. This footnote-catalogue starts off with a statement that speaks obliquely of Boswell's own project: 'As no inconsiderable circumstance of his fame, we must reckon the extraordinary zeal of the artists to extend and perpetuate his [Johnson's]

[30] Though these remarks are ill judged in the context of verbal portraiture, they do reveal Boswell's struggle to document, and to come to terms with, an unreconstructed version of his subject. See Ch. 5 below.

[31] *Boswell in Search of a Wife 1766–1769*, ed. Frank Brady and Frederick A. Pottle (London: Heinemann, 1957), 311 (16 Sept. 1769).

image.' In order 'to extend and perpetuate' his version of that image, Boswell proceeds to delete the subdivisions ('religious moral political and literary') he had taken over from the *Tour*: these categories intrude an arbitrary schema that works against the unity of the portrait. He refines the key verb in the introductory paragraph—starting with 'sum up', combining it with 'collect', discarding both in favour of 'bring together', and settling at the proof stage on 'collect into one view' (Fig. 2). He adds (also at proof stage) two sentences that describe Johnson-in-motion:

but when he walked, it was like the struggling gait of one in fetters; when he rode he had no command or direction of his horse, but was carried as if in a balloon. That with his constitution and habits of life he should have lived seventy-five years, is a proof that an inherent *vivida vis* is a powerful preservative of the human frame.

These sentences complete the description of Johnson by conveying a sense of his massive, ungainly, but vigorous body—a body that is as scarred yet as heroic as his mind. By reducing the quotation from Lucretius—'vivida vis animi' or 'lively power of mind'— to 'vivida vis' alone, Boswell attaches 'lively power' to both body and mind.[32] This connection is cemented by the phrase 'native vigour of the mind' that appears early in the following paragraph. For similar reasons, Boswell adds the prepositional phrase 'in a vigorous sense' to the sentence that incorporates a quotation from Luke: '"Of him to whom much is given much will be required" seems to have been ever present to his mind.'[33] In these various ways, he supports and extends the mind–body connection and through it the coherence of his portrait.

---

[32] Boswell uses the same tag (*De Rerum Natura* I. 72) in letters to Wilkes and Burke (Baker, 132).

[33] 'In a vigorous sense' is the reading of the revises; the 1st edition, however, prints 'in a rigorous sense'. Is this an error or a last-minute revision?

The quotation from Luke is followed by one from 1 Corinthians: 'If in this life only he had hope, he was of all men the most miserable.' In the manuscript, Boswell goes on to comment, 'But I trust that he has now more benignant views of the divine administration and is participating in the happiness of the just' (MS 1042^v). This rather sanctimonious observation not only diverts attention from subject to biographer; it also shifts the frame of reference from the terrestrial to the celestial, disembodying Johnson at just the point we are being asked to visualize him most concretely. It is a measure of Boswell's editorial self-scrutiny that this sentence has vanished by the stage of proof, and that the Character moves directly from Johnson's melancholy to his love of praise.

Boswell likewise strengthens the links between verbal and visual portraiture in a final footnote, which connects his Character to Clarendon's account of Lord Falkland. Boswell attends carefully to the beginning of this footnote, recasting the first clause so that 'a perfect resemblance of Johnson' replaces 'a full parallel to Johnson' (MS 1044). But it is the final sentence of the Character that drives home the full import of 'resemblance'. That sentence (which of course concludes the entire biography as well) acquires an epitaphic force from being separately paragraphed.[34] It acquires an epigrammatic force from a dense clusters of puns: 'the more that we consider his character, we

[34] In MS, revises, and 1st edition, the final sentence reads: '. . . and in all his numerous works he earnestly inculcated what appeared to him to be the truth. His piety was constant, and was the ruling principle of all his conduct; and the more we consider his character, we shall be the more disposed to regard him with admiration and reverence.' The 2nd edition prints: 'and, in all his numerous works, he earnestly inculcated what appeared to him to be the truth; his piety being constant, and the ruling principle of all his conduct. [Paragraph Break] Such was SAMUEL JOHNSON, a man whose talents, acquirements, and virtues, were so extraordinary, that the more his character is considered, the more he will be regarded by the present age, and by posterity, with admiration and reverence.'

shall be the more disposed to regard him with admiration and reverence.' In preparing the second edition, Boswell remakes the sentence so that it reads, 'the more his character is considered, the more he will be regarded by the present age, and by posterity, with admiration and reverence.' The first version is the stronger, for it clinches more emphatically the reader's spectatorial relationship to the biographical portrait. But in both versions Boswell activates the multiple meanings of 'character', 'consider', and 'regard', as defined in Johnson's *Dictionary*. Three senses of 'character' are called into play: 'a mark, a stamp, a representation'; 'a representation of any man as to his personal qualities'; 'personal qualities; particular constitution of the mind'. To 'consider' Johnson's character is 'to think upon [it] with care, to ponder, to examine', and also 'to take [it] into the view'—a meaning that tallies with the 'collect into one view' that introduced us to the portrait. The word that might be said to sum up not only Boswell's goal but his method is the final verb in the *Life*: 'regard'. All but one of Johnson's seven definitions apply: 'to value', 'to observe', 'to observe religiously', 'to pay attention to', 'to respect', and 'to look towards'. We complete the Character and close the biography understanding that our regard *for* Johnson depends upon our regard *of* him—that vision has led to veneration. According to David Piper, panegyrists from the fifteenth century onward 'have always praised the painter for his power not merely to consider but positively to realize the whole character or the essential soul of the sitter. . . . To portray in short, not merely the sitter's identity, but his entity.'[35] It is Boswell's culminating achievement to unite the two, to create out of multiple transactions with both his subject and his dedicatee a portrait for which the label 'Flemish' is no

[35] Piper, 'The Development of the British Literary Portrait up to Samuel Johnson', *Proceedings of the British Academy*, 54 (1968), 52.

longer remotely sufficient. What biographer-painter (Boswell) and painter-biographer (Reynolds) were up to, and what they ask of us, is best conveyed by Boswell's journal entry for 1 September 1792. Reynolds had died six months before, and Boswell was beginning to work on the second edition of the *Life*. Standing before Reynolds's final self-portrait, he observes: 'It has a sort of *pulled-up* look, and not the placid gentleness of his smiling manner; but the features, though rather too largely and strongly limned, are most exactly portrayed, and the dress in every respect being such as he usually wore, I think it the best representation of my celebrated friend.'[36]

[36] *Great Biographer*, 170.

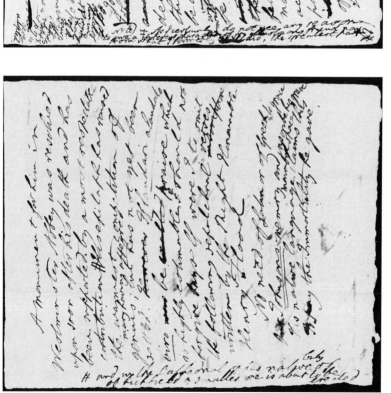

Figs. 1 and 2. MS leaves 1037^v and 1038^r: in keeping with the compositional method he had adopted at the outset, Boswell has drafted his narrative on the recto and used the facing verso for additions and/or revisions.

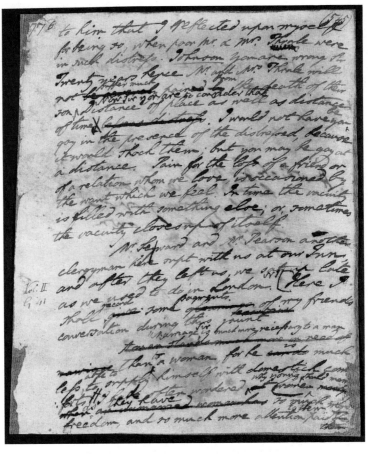

FIG. 3. MS leaf 545^r: the signature mark (designating Sheet G
of volume ii) appears in the lower left-hand margin.

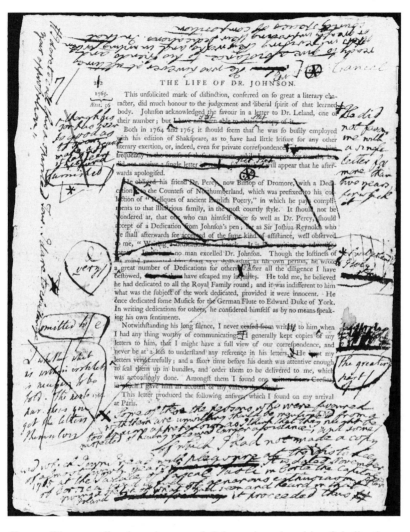

Fig. 4. The cancellandum that reveals Johnson's authorship of dedications for both Reynolds and Percy; Boswell has supplied the text for the cancellans at the top of the page.

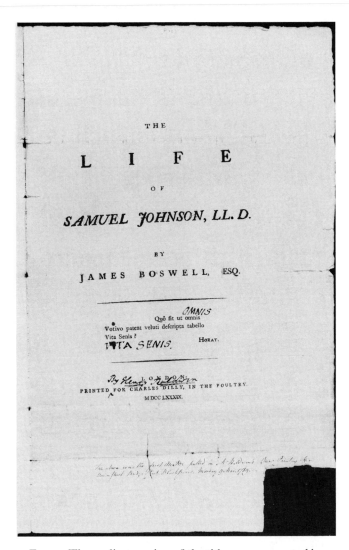

Fig. 5. The earliest version of the title page, corrected by
Boswell and annotated by Thomas Edlyne Tomlins:
'The above was the first Matter pulled in Mr. Baldwin's
New Printing Office, Union street Bridge Street
Blackfriars. Monday 9 Mar. 1789'.

FIG. 6. The frontispiece to the first edition:
James Heath's engraving of Sir Joshua Reynolds's
earliest known portrait of Johnson.

This is the first impression of the Plate
after Mr Heath the Engraver thought it was
finished. He went with me to Sir Joshua Reynolds's
who suggested that the countenance was too
young and not thoughtful enough. Mr Heath
therefore altered it so much to its advantage that
Sir Joshua was quite satisfied, and Heath then saw such
a difference that he said he would not for a hundred
pounds have had it remain as it was.

FIGS. 7 and 8. The second and third states of James Heath's engraving
of the portrait by Sir Joshua Reynolds; in his annotations, Boswell
emphasizes Reynolds's role in 'improving' the second state,
which Boswell mistakenly calls the first.

Second Impression of D^r. Johnson's Portrait
after the Plate had been improved by Sir
Joshua Reynolds's suggestions. Mr Heath
afterwards gave it a few additional
touches.

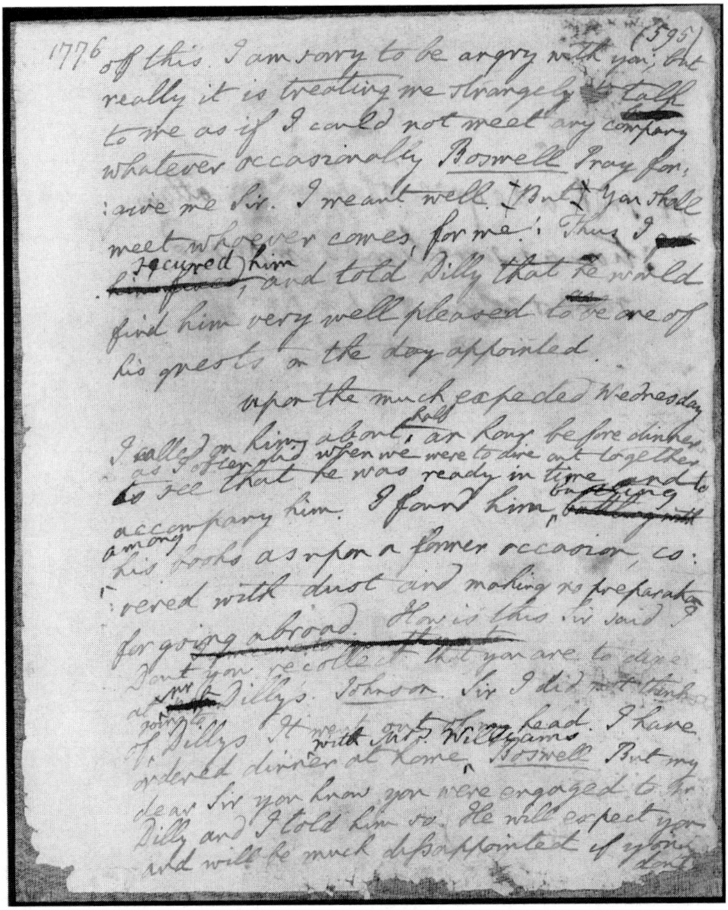
1776 of this. I am sorry to be angry with you; but
really it is treating me strangely to talk
to me as if I could not meet any company
whatever occasionally Boswell I pray for:
:give me Sir. I meant well. [But] You shall
meet whoever comes, for me. Thus I
secured him and told Dilly that he would
find him very well pleased to be one of
his guests on the day appointed.
Upon the much expected Wednesday
I called on him about half an hour before dinner
as I often did when we were to dine out together
to see that he was ready in time and to
accompany him. I found him bustling
among his books as upon a former occasion, co:
:vered with dust and making no preparation
for going abroad. How is this Sir said I
Dont you recollect that you are to dine
at Mr Dilly's. Johnson Sir I did not think
of going to Dilly's. It went out of my head. I have
ordered dinner at home with Mrs Williams. Boswell But my
dear Sir you know you were engaged to Mr
Dilly and I told him so. He will expect you
and will be much disappointed if you dont

FIG. 9. MS leaf 595r: in a much-celebrated passage, part of the playlet dramatizing the first meeting between Johnson and Wilkes, the verb 'buffeting' results from a compositorial misreading of Boswell's 'bustling'.

3

Dramatizing Johnson

Within days of deciding to draw Johnson 'in the style of a Flemish painter', Boswell returns to the visual arts for a second provocative comparison: 'He and I were both in high spirits, and talked keenly. It is impossible to put down an exact transcript of conversation with all its little particulars. It is impossible to clap the mind upon paper as one does an engraved plate, and to leave the full vivid impression.'[1] Boswell the diarist had long been haunted by the gap between sensation and documentation: 'I should live no more than I can record, as one should not have more corn growing than one can get in.'[2] Boswell the biographer faces an even more daunting challenge: he must not only capture the evanescent, he must do justice to someone who 'talked *keenly*' in both senses of the adverb ('avidly' and 'incisively'). Boswell needs, in short, to find a way of turning that which is wholly wit into that which is wholly writ.

As he recognizes, it is indeed 'impossible to clap [Johnson's] mind upon paper'. Nevertheless, Boswell takes on the challenge. His medium is the engraving of conversation. The journal makes it clear that his ideal is an 'exact transcript', a 'full vivid impression'. Because this transcript can never be 'exact', this impression 'full', the record must be as 'vivid' as possible. Yet how can Boswell convert into biographical substance the human essence

<hr />

[1] *Boswell: The Ominous Years 1774–1776*, ed. Charles Ryskamp and Frederick A. Pottle (New York: McGraw-Hill, 1963), 133 (7 Apr. 1775). It is possible that Boswell, who thought of both Jonson and Johnson as 'celebrated wits', was remembering the conceit that underlies Jonson's prefatory poem to the first folio of Shakespeare's *Works*. See *Life* v. 402–3.

[2] *Ominous Years*, ed. Ryskamp and Pottle, 265 (17 Mar. 1776).

that he labels, with help from Lucretius, Johnson's *vivida vis*—his 'lively power' of mind and tongue?

The solution suggests itself eight years into the project: he will 'write Dr. Johnson's life in scenes'.[3] After beginning to compose the biography, Boswell expanded upon this idea in a letter to Thomas Percy: 'It appears to me that mine is the best plan of Biography that can be conceived; for my Readers will as near as may be accompany Johnson in his progress, and as it were see each scene as it happened.'[4] This statement adumbrates the introduction to the *Life*, which Boswell composed after he had completed the body of the text:

> Indeed I cannot conceive a more perfect mode of writing any man's life, than not only relating all the most important events of it in their order, but interweaving what he privately wrote, and said, and thought, by which Mankind are enabled as it were to see him live and to 'live o'er each scene' with him. . . . What I consider as the peculiar value of the following Work, is the quantity that it contains of Johnson's conversation . . . That the conversation of a celebrated man, if his talents have been exerted in conversation, will best display his character, is I trust too well established in the judgement of mankind to be at all shaken by a sneering observation of Mr. Mason in his Memoirs of Mr. William Whitehead, in which there is literally no *Life*, but a mere dry narrative of facts. (*Life MS* i. 10–11)

Boswell 'displays' Johnson's 'character' and causes us to 'see him live' not only by pictorializing but by dramatizing—by setting his protagonist in motion within a sequence of carefully scripted playlets. He signals his intention by quoting part of a couplet from Pope's prologue to Addison's *Cato*: 'To make mankind, in conscious virtue bold, | Live o'er each scene, and be what they

---

³ *Boswell, Laird of Auchinleck 1778–1782*, ed. Joseph W. Reed and Frederick A. Pottle (New York: McGraw-Hill, 1977), 260 (12 Oct. 1780).

⁴ *The Correspondence of James Boswell with Certain Members of The Club*, ed. Charles N. Fifer (New York: McGraw-Hill, 1976), 258 (Boswell to Percy, 9 Feb. 1788).

behold.'[5] This couplet not only exhorts the audience to emulate the worthy protagonist; it also suggests that the key to the didactic exercise ('to make mankind, in conscious virtue bold') is the absorption of spectator into spectacle ('live o'er each scene, and be what they behold').

Boswell understood that Johnson, for all his strictures against players and play-acting, was himself a consummate performer. He practised, perfected, and strove to institutionalize through the Literary Club a highly theatrical kind of conversation. As on so many other topics, Johnson had thought carefully about the theory behind his practice:

Of conversation he said, 'There must in the first place be knowledge; there must be materials. In the second place, there must be a command of words. In the third place, there must be imagination to place things in such views as they are not commonly seen. And in the fourth place, there must be presence of mind and a resolution which is not to be overcome by failures.'[6]

The greatest conversational set-pieces in the *Life* are precisely those that fulfil these Johnsonian prerequisites. The talk is substantive, fluent, and competitive; it exhibits a conscious virtuosity that never lapses into preciosity. In order to recreate the aura as well as the substance of such talk, Boswell shapes his raw materials into a succession of scenic arcs. As the quotation from Pope suggests, these arcs are designed to turn beholding into being, as the essential (and inspirational) Johnson imprints himself upon the reader.

The raw materials for the *Life* confirm and enhance the testimony of the manuscript: Boswell devoted his primary efforts

---

[5] 'Prologue to Mr. Addison's *Cato*', in *The Poems of Alexander Pope*, ed. John Butt (New Haven: Yale University Press, 1963), 211.

[6] *Boswell: The Applause of the Jury 1782–1785*, ed. Irma S. Lustig and Frederick A. Pottle (New York: McGraw-Hill, 1981), 75 (21 Mar. 1783).

to recording not isolated sayings but sayings-in-context. These efforts begin immediately after the initial encounter at Tom Davies's, when he 'preserved the following short minute without marking the [connecting *del*] questions and observations by which it was [produced/drawn out>] produced' (*Life MS* i. 270). It is ironic that the words Boswell discards, 'connecting' and 'drawn out', should help us to grasp the importance of conversation as a vital explanatory matrix for Johnsonian *mots*. This function emerges even more strongly from a revealing aside that Boswell plants midway through the narrative for 1773: 'Much pleasant conversation passed which Johnson [relished/seemed to relish>] relished with great good humour. But [his conversation alone/only his sayings>] his conversation alone or what led to [it/them] it or was interwoven with it [that *del*] is the business of this [record>] work' (*Life MS* ii. 104).

In order to win the trust of the potentially sceptical reader, Boswell describes what amounts to a biographical apprenticeship, during which he masters his craft as a reporter of conversation:

Let me here once for all [lament how imperfectly I have preserved the remembrance/how defective my record is of such conversation, as if completely recollected would be the richest treasure. But I hope I shall be allowed credit for the diligence which has preserved so much of it.>] apologise for the imperfect manner in which I am obliged to exhibit his conversation at this period. In the early [part/period>] part of my acquaintance with Johnson, I was so rapt in admiration of his extraordinary colloquial talents, and so little accustomed to his peculiar mode of expression that I found it [very difficult to write down with its genuine flavour what I had heard him say>] extremely difficult to recollect and record his conversation with its genuine vigour and vivacity. (*Life MS* i. 291)

Boswell's first version of this passage is abject in tone: it 'lament[s]' his inadequacy and mourns his impartial recovery of 'the richest treasure'. The revisions temper these keen regrets into an apology for what is not so much radically inadequate as regrettably 'imperfect'. Within months of the first meeting, moreover, Boswell is not only remembering, he is confidently shaping what he remembers:

We staid so long at Greenwich that our sail up the river in our return to London was by no means so pleasant as in the morning ... the night air was so cold that [I shivered in the boat>] it made me shiver. ₍ₐ₎I [was the more sensible of it/felt it the more that I had sat/been up all the former night recollecting and recording in my Journal the scenes and conversations of the foregoing/preceding day>] was the more sensible of it from having sat up all the night before recollecting and writing in my Journal what I thought worthy of preservation.₍ₐ₎ (*Life MS* i. 323–4)

The original version of this passage quietly forecasts the mode that will soon be dominating the biography: 'scenes and conversations'.

The sources of life in the *Life* are various: they include the gallery of portraits we have just been considering, and the array of letters that forms the subject of the next chapter. But no feature of the biography is more *vital*, in more senses than one, than the conversation-pieces. In fact we tend to remember the biography, especially on first reading, as a glorious anthology of scenes. Boswell elicits this response by lavishing all his arts on sustained exercises in conversational polyphony—the most ambitious of which repay the closest attention.[7] Yet there are scores of less intricate conversations that do almost as much to

[7] My musical terminology acknowledges Boswell's own wish to notate Johnson's talk: 'His tone in speaking was indeed very impressive, and I wish it could be preserved as musick is written, according to the very ingenious method of Mr. Steele in his "System of intonation as applied to language" in which that of Mr. Garrick and other eminent speakers is if I may use the expression put *in score*' (*Life MS* ii. 140–1).

make us 'live o'er each scene'. To create these chamber pieces, most of which originate in his journal, Boswell makes expert use of two basic moves: deletion and interpolation. Only the *Life* manuscript can reveal what he changes and why he changes it. Before moving on to the virtuoso ensembles, let us consider five examples of Boswell at work on a small scale.

Duets and Trios

When they meet on 27 March 1768, Boswell and Johnson engage in a short-lived but intense dispute. The point at issue concerns 'the pleasing system of brutes existing in the other world', a system that Boswell 'wanted much to defend'.[8] With characteristic doubleness, he splits into an actor who struggles and a narrator who stands apart, observing his own 'serious, metaphysical, pensive face' as he 'venture[s] to say, "But really, Sir, when we see a very sensible dog, we know not what to think of him." '[9] In the original account, Johnson behaves like *Ursa Major*—a bear who, 'growling with joy', 'bounced along . . . laughing and exulting over me': 'No, Sir; and when we see a very foolish fellow, we don't know what to think of him.' But it is Boswell who has the last word: 'I took it to myself and had only to say, "Well, but you do not know what to think of a very sensible dog." '

As he begins to incorporate this episode into the biography, Boswell decides to conceal his identity behind the mask of 'a Gentleman . . . who seemed fond of curious speculation' (*Life*

[8] *Boswell in Search of a Wife 1766–1769*, ed. Frank Brady and Frederick A. Pottle (London: Heinemann, 1957), 164 (27 Mar. 1768).

[9] The classic study of this split is Bertrand H. Bronson's essay 'Boswell's Boswell', in *'Johnson Agonistes' and Other Essays* (Berkeley and Los Angeles: Univ. of California Press, 1965), 53–99.

MS ii. 28). He tempers the aggressive physicality of Johnson's reaction by turning 'growling with joy' into 'rowling with joy', and 'bounced' into 'strided'; moreover, Johnson's 'joy' is now said to 'beam in his eye'. As a consequence of these changes, benevolence and a sense of the ludicrous peek through the bearish behaviour. But the decisive alteration occurs when Boswell deletes his final retort: '[The Gentleman did not shrink; but when the merriment was/had abated gravely persevered saying "ᴧWellᴧ But you Sir do not know what to think of a very sensible dog." *del*]' (*Life MS* ii. 28). This deletion keeps the exchange from degenerating into petulance, allows Johnson to have the last word, and sustains the serio-comic tone of the episode.

Johnson the talker-for-victory likewise emerges undimmed from a reshaped conversation at Streatham Park:

Mrs. Thrale disputed with him on the merit of Prior. He attacked him powerfully, said he wrote of love like a man who had never felt it. His love verses were College verses. And he repeated the Song Alexis shunned his fellow swains [so ludicrously>] . . . in so ludicrous a manner [that he made us laugh very heartily, and wonder>] as to make us all wonder how any body could have been [seriously *del*] pleased with such fantastical stuff. Mrs. Thrale stood to her gun with great courage in defence of amorous ditties which Johnson despised till he at last silenced her by saying, 'My Dear Lady talk no more of this. Nonsense can be defended but by nonsense.' [This was in a great measure/degree a sportive attack; for in his Life of Prior he has given him deserved praise. *del*] (*Life MS* ii. 41)

Had Boswell retained his original ending, he would have complicated, and thereby diffused, the effect of the dispute by quoting Johnson against himself. The vividness of the account depends upon the reader's ability to remain within the scene: to experience the push and pull, the unqualified force of Johnson's pronouncements, and the silencing of Hester Thrale. The final deletion helps us to understand anew that Boswell will always subordinate Johnson the writer (and the complex sense of the author that emerges from his work) to Johnson the social performer.

As in the two examples we have just been considering, Boswell's decision to delete material at the end of a paragraph tends to create the effect of a crescendo: the scene reaches its climax and conclusion in the double double double beat of the thund'ring Johnsonian drum. Occasionally, however, Boswell will remove material that not only undercuts a resounding close but also diminishes the twin illusions of biographical completeness and dramatic transparency:

Johnson. Burton's Anatomy of Melancholy is a valuable Work. It is perhaps overloaded with quotation. But there is great spirit and great power in what Burton says when he writes from his own mind. [How much do I regret that I had not diligence enough to record/preserve/ register all his conversation this evening/night the recollection of which consoles my mind. *del*] (*Life MS* ii. 192)

Thanks to the disappearance of Boswell's subjective commentary, we feel that we are privileged eavesdroppers, who have overheard the conversation freshly and overheard it completely.

Deletions in the middle of a conversational block occur less frequently than those at the end of a paragraph, but their effect is no less pronounced. As Boswell drafts the account of a breakfast meeting at William Strahan's, his first thought is to inset two conversations within the scene: as the three men talk, Johnson mentions an encounter with Mrs Abington, which Boswell then links to similar speeches before moving back to the primary conversation:

He told us that he was engaged to go [at night/that evening>] that evening to Mrs. Abington's benefit. 'She was visiting some Ladies whom I was visiting, and begged that I would come to her benefit. I told her I could not hear. But she insisted so much on my coming, that it would have been brutal to have refused her.' This was a speech quite characteristical. [He did not mention the Ladies whom he was visiting. He loved to be mysterious in little matters. He used to say 'I am to dine at the other end of the town. I am to dine near Grosvenor Square,' so that we might suppose that it was with a Duke. And he was vain of a fine actress's solicitations. He said the Play was to be the Hypocrite, altered from Cibber's Nonjuror. He said>] (*Life MS* ii. 137)

In the course of revision, Boswell retains the first inset conversation but eliminates the second, replacing it with an indulgent comment on Johnson's social behaviour: 'He loved to bring forward his having been in the gay circles of life. And he was perhaps a little vain of the solicitations of this elegant and fashionable actress' (*Life MS* ii. 137). In making this change Boswell not only avoids the imputation to Johnson of Goldsmithian strutting and snobbery; he also sustains the momentum of the primary conversation, which might have been disrupted by too much interpolation. The result is a clear gain in dramatic focus and control of sympathy.

Amongst the most absorbing patterns of revision are those that combine deletion and substitution throughout a given dialogue. When Boswell remakes a conversation that takes Lord Auchinleck as its point of departure, he faces the challenge of retaining vividness while upholding decorum:

[BOSWELL.] 'Nobody content.' DR. JOHNSON. 'No, Sir.' BOSWELL. 'Yes, my father.' JOHNSON. 'No, Sir. He has always some scheme, some new plantation. When your mother died, was not content, but married again.' BOSWELL. 'But he is not restless.' JOHNSON. 'Sir, he's locally at rest. A chemist is locally at rest, yet his mind is working hard. Your father has done with external wishes. He cannot get more.' BOSWELL. 'But he scrapes books for three hours.' JOHNSON. 'Yes, Sir. But he's thinking of something else.'[10]

---

[10] *Boswell in Extremes 1776–1778*, ed. Charles McC. Weis and Frederick A. Pottle (New York: McGraw-Hill, 1970), 245 (7 Apr. 1778).

Boswell's first move is to turn Lord Auchinleck into 'a respect-able Person in Scotland', who no longer 'scrapes books for three hours' but 'seems to . . . amuse himself quite well, to have his attention fixed, and his tranquillity preserved by very small matters' (MS 641–2). Contrary to his usual practice, which is to add stage directions as he reshapes a conversation, Boswell takes them out: '*Boswell.* So it will be said "Once for his amuse-ment he tried knotting. Nor did this Hercules disdain the Distaff [(He and Mrs. Desmoulins both laughing heartily) *del.*]. Once for his amusement he tried knotting"' (MS 643). But the most significant deletion occurs when Boswell removes the exchange that originally ended the conversation:

BOSWELL. 'I should like to have seen you play on violoncello. *That* should have been *your* instrument.' JOHNSON. 'Sir, I might as well have played on violoncello as another. But I should have done nothing else.'[11]

The excision of this final bit of dialogue leaves the reader imagin-ing Johnson the Scottish knitter rather than Johnson the obses-sive cellist: '*Johnson* "Knitting of stockings is a good amusement. As a freeman of Aberdeen I should be a knitter"' (MS 643). This picture is doubly incongruous and therefore especially piquant.

As part of his reshaping of small-scale conversations, Boswell not only deletes, he also conflates. An occasional brief aside alerts the reader to this practice: '∧Sometimes∧ short notes of different days shall be blended together and sometimes a day may seem important enough to be separately distinguished' (*Life MS* ii. 37). However, such bland remarks do almost nothing to tip Boswell's hand; in fact, I would argue, they are intended to cover him as he boldly 'blend[s] together' his raw materials. The governing purpose is usually to create or sustain a unified conversation—but scenic biography can sometimes shade into tacit polemic, as in Boswell's handling of remarks about Edward Gibbon. On their trip to Oxford in 1776, the topic of the newly published *Decline and Fall* surfaces repeatedly. In the manuscript Boswell creates one scene out of two by silently folding his rejoinder to John Smith, a don 'who indecently talks as an unbeliever', into a conversation with Johnson that took place after the meeting with Smith.[12] As he quarries the journal, moreover, Boswell changes his warning against the *Decline and Fall* from 'Springs and traps set here' to 'Spring-guns and mantraps set here' (*Life MS* ii. 196). He also adds a sentence to Johnson's sardonic commentary on Gibbon's religious history: 'It is said that his range has been more [varied>] extensive, and that he has once been Mahometan' (*Life MS* ii. 196). The combined effect of these moves is to unite biographer and protagonist even more strongly in opposition to Gibbon's 'Bolus . . . of infidelity'.[13]

Virtuoso Polyphony

As a moralist, Johnson was keenly aware of the gap between ideal code and actual conduct; as a practising critic, he constantly violated, complicated, or undercut his own theoretical pronouncements. So too his talk about talk can seem almost disingenuously wide of the mark:

He [said>] was pleased to say 'If you come to settle here, we will have one day in the week on which we will meet by ourselves. That is the happiest conversation where there is no competition no vanity, but a [quiet/calm/fair>] calm quiet interchange of sentiments.' (*Life MS* ii. 159)

Boswell may well have decided to discard 'fair' because he

---

[12] See *Ominous Years*, ed. Ryskamp and Pottle, 282–3 (20–1 Mar. 1776).
[13] This reading does not survive the final round of revision.

wished to eliminate a potentially misleading ambiguity: conversations with Johnson, however 'gentle', could not also be
described as 'equal'.[14] But if any can be accurately judged free
of 'competition' and 'vanity', it is the intimate exchanges we
have just been considering. The polyphonic conversations, by
contrast, are always marked by virtuoso combat. We can situate
such conversations in what Alvin Kernan has called 'that semi-
private world of talk which is located between the fully public
scene of oratory and the totally private scene of reading'.[15] At
the same time, we must grant that they move much closer than
the duets and trios to 'the fully public scene of oratory'—witness
their length, complexity, and sophistication.

Our ability to make meaningful comparisons across the
rhetorical spectrum is a direct result of Boswell's ability to adjust
means to mode. As we juxtapose notes and journal entries to the
manuscript we come to suspect Paul Korshin's sweeping claim:
'A thorough comparison of the longer conversations in the *Life*
with their earlier form . . . reveals that Boswell almost always
transfers the earlier long form of a conversation to the *Life* without significant changes.'[16] Far from 'transfer[ring] . . . without
significant changes', Boswell pulls out all the stops, demonstrat-
ing in text that very 'imagination' and 'command' that Johnson
had called for in talk.

For his account of a dinner at Allan Ramsay's, Boswell devises
a sophisticated tripartite format, which frames the central conversation with two scenes: the first prepares for the entrance of

[14] These are definitions 12 and 8 respectively in Johnson's *Dictionary* (4th edn.,
1773).

[15] Alvin Kernan, *Printing Technology, Letters & Samuel Johnson* (Princeton: Princeton Univ. Press, 1987), 206.

[16] Paul J. Korshin, 'Johnson's Conversation in Boswell's *Life of Johnson*', in
Greg Clingham (ed.), *New Light on Boswell* (Cambridge: Cambridge Univ. Press,
1991), 178.

Johnson, the second offers a post-mortem that clinches the principal point at issue. In the preliminary scene, Boswell, Ramsay, William Robertson, and Joshua Reynolds behave like courtiers who are debating the character and conduct of their prince. Each testifies out of his own experience:

Before Dr. Johnson came, we talked of him. Ramsay said he had always found him a very polite man, and he treated him with great respect, which he did very sincerely. I said I worshipped him. Robertson said, 'But some of you spoil him. You should not worship him. You should worship no man.' Said I, 'I cannot help worshipping him. He is so much superior to other men.' (Let Robertson take this.)[17]

As he recasts his journal entry, Boswell softens the asperity of Robertson's remark by inserting a speech that describes the historian's first meeting with Johnson:

Robertson. 'He and I have been allways very gracious. The first time I met him was one evening at Strahan's, when he had just had an unlucky altercation with Adam Smith to whom he had been so rough that Strahan after Smith was gone had remonstrated with him and told him that I was coming soon and that he was uneasy to think that he might behave in the same manner to me.' 'No no Sir' said Johnson. 'I warrant you Robertson and I shall do very well.' Accordingly he was gentle and good humoured and courteous with me the whole evening; and he has been so upon every occasion that we have met since. (MS 733)

Robertson's testimony not only tempers his initial objection to 'spoiling' Johnson, it also prepares for the issue that will dominate the entire episode: what is the relationship, if any, between Johnson's social and his literary conduct?

Shortly before Johnson arrives, Boswell and Reynolds discuss his powers as a verbal portraitist:

Boswell. 'His power of reasoning is very strong, and he has a peculiar

---

[17] *Boswell in Extremes*, ed. Weis and Pottle, 322 (29 Apr. 1778).

art of drawing characters which is as rare as good portrait painting.'
Sir Joshua Reynolds. 'He is undoubtedly admirable in this; but in order
to mark the characters which he draws he overcharges them, and gives
people more than they really have, whether of good or bad.' (MS 733)

And so the introductory scene ends as it has begun, in polite but
provocative disagreement. The consequence is that, even 700
pages into the biography, our curiosity is piqued afresh: whose
assessment will Johnson's behaviour, as actor and as analyst, go
on to confirm? Boswell enlists us as witnesses and interpreters,
who will 'mark' Johnson marking character.

Boswell introduces the central scene with a comparison that
clinches our understanding of what has gone before and creates
the atmosphere for what is to follow: '[When/No sooner was the
great Man arrived>] No sooner did he of whom we had been
thus talking so easily arrive, than we were all as quiet as a school
upon the entrance of the Head Master' (MS 734). The comparison strikes home, in part because Johnson duly proceeds to
behave like a schoolmaster in a classroom. His pupils are accom-
plished, but they remain pupils nonetheless. The headmaster
contradicts, he qualifies, he admonishes, he discourses on multiple topics: Pope's poetry, modern literature, antiquarianism,
abstinence, Robert Adam, Lord Clive. Boswell heightens the *ex
cathedra* quality of these dicta by balancing Johnson's clauses and
making his diction less colloquial:

We must read what the World reads [for/at>] at the [time>] moment.
It has been maintained that the superfoetation this teeming of the press
in [modern times/modern days/these days>] modern times [hurts>]
is prejudicial to good literature because it [makes us have>] obliges
us to read so much of ∧what is of∧ inferiour value [to read from fash-
ion>] in order to be in the fashion so that better works are neglected for
want of time because a man will have more gratification of ∧his∧ vanity
in conversation [who has/from having>] from having read modern

books than [who has/from having>] from having read [better/the best>] the best works of antiquity. (MS 734–5)

At a late stage of revision, this speech is rounded off with the most incisive of epigrams: 'Greece appears to me to be the fountain of knowledge, Rome of elegance' (MS 735).

When the conversation turns to Robert Adam and Lord Clive, Robertson offers 'characters' of both. In his responses to these portraits, Johnson demonstrates his superior powers by adding to the historian's command of fact the moralist's ability to generalize from the particular:

Dr. Robertson expatiated on the character of [an eminent/great man/general>] a certain great general—that he was one of the strongest-minded men that ever lived; that he would sit in [a *del*] company quite sluggish, while there was nothing to call [forth/out>] forth his vigour of mind; but the moment that any important subject was started, for instance how this country is to be defended against a french invasion he would rouse himself and shew his [great>] extraordinary talents with the [utmost/most powerful>] most powerful ability and animation. *Johnson.* Yet this man cut his own throat. The true strong and sound mind is the mind that can [equally embrace/embrace equally>] embrace equally great things and small. . . . [An ingenious gentleman/Mr. Robert Adam architect>] An ingenious gentleman was mentioned [as to whom/who>] concerning whom both Robertson and Ramsay agreed that he had a constant firmness of mind; for after a laborious day and amidst a multiplicity of cares and anxieties he could sit down with his sisters and be quite cheerful and good=humoured. Such a disposition it was observed was a happy gift of nature. *Johnson.* I do not think so. A man has from nature/naturally[18] a certain portion of mind; the use he makes of [which/it>] it depends upon [his will/himself>] his own free will. (MS 736–7)

Boswell invites us to understand that Johnson exemplifies both

---

[18] The alternative phrasing is not resolved in the MS. By the time of revises, 'from nature' had been selected.

generalizations, that his mind as it manifests itself in such talk is 'true', 'strong', 'sound', and 'free'. Our admiration is clinched by the following day's post-mortem, when Johnson delivers a concise 'character' of their host: 'Well Sir Ramsay gave us a splendid dinner. [Ramsay is a fine fellow>] I love Ramsay. You will not find a man in whose conversation there is more instruction more information and more elegance than [in Ramsays/that of Ramsay>] in Ramsays' (MS 738). This declaration, which sends us back to the opening scene, completes Boswell's enterprise in three ways: it supports his opinion about Johnson's 'peculiar art of drawing characters'; it shows Johnson to be more judicious than Robertson; and it unites acuity of judgement with generosity of spirit, thereby confirming the 'character' of Johnson himself that was sketched before his arrival.

Johnson plays the role of schoolmaster to somewhat different effect at a dinner given by Eva Maria Garrick—the first time she had entertained since her husband's death, Boswell is careful to tell us. Though his notes provide the scaffolding, he turns to Shakespeare for help in recreating 'one of the most agreable days that I can remember to have enjoyed in the whole course of my life' (MS 828). Boswell sets the stage for this *ne plus ultra* of evenings by quoting from Johnson's tribute to Garrick in his 'Life of Edmund Smith': 'We found ourselves very elegantly entertained at her house in the Adelphi where I have [enjoyed>] passed many a pleasing hour with him "who gladdened life" ' (MS 828).[19] He then makes special mention of two portraits—

---

[19] The phrase in question comes from a paragraph that may have guided Boswell as he strove to combine gaiety and pathos in this conversation: 'At this man's table I enjoyed many chearful and instructive hours, with companions such as are not often found: with one who has lengthened and one who has gladdened life; with Dr. James, whose skill in physick will be long remembered; and with David Garrick, whom I hoped to have gratified with this character of our common friend: but what are the hopes of man! I am disappointed by that stroke

one that dominates Eva Maria Garrick's drawing room and one
that belongs to Topham Beauclerk:

[She] Talked of her husband with complacency, and while she cast her
eye on [the>] his portrait which hung over the chimneypiece said
that 'death was now the most agreable [thought>] [idea>] object to
her.' The very [appearance>] semblance of David Garrick was cheer-
ing. Mr. Beauclerk with happy propriety inscribed under [that/his>]
that fine portrait of him which by Lady Diana's kindness is now the
property of my friend ∧Mr.∧ Langton the following passage from his
[divine>] [favourite>] [immortal>] beloved Shakespeare

A merrier man
(three lines) (MS 828–9)

The lines in question come from Rosaline's speech at the begin-
ning of Act II of *Love's Labour's Lost*: 'but a merrier man, |
Within the limit of becoming mirth, | I never spent an hour's
talk withal.' By the time of revised proof, Boswell had decided
to include the rest of the speech, which praises the 'sweet and
voluble . . . discourse' of Berowne.[20] By conjuring up the two
images of the dead actor, and supplying the full Shakespearian
quotation, Boswell helps to convey the emotionally complex
atmosphere of the evening, whose conversational buoyancy (like
that of *Love's Labour's Lost*) is tinged with sadness. Even before
it begins, talk has come to figure as the vehicle both for joyful
celebration and for elegiac commemoration.

As he cuts, expands, and reorders, Boswell shapes a conversational sequence that emphasizes Johnson's Garrick-like wit
and assimilates itself to the 'sweet and voluble . . . discourse' of

of death, which has eclipsed the gaiety of nations, and impoverished the publick
stock of harmless pleasure' ('Edmund Smith', from *Lives of the Poets*, ed. G. B. Hill
(Oxford: Clarendon Press, 1905), ii. 21).

[20] Shakespeare, *The Complete Works*, ed. Alfred Harbage (Baltimore: Penguin
Books, 1969), 184–5 (II. i. 66–8, 76).

Rosaline's encomium. The sequence begins with a toast consolidating the link between Garrick and Johnson:

> In addition to a splendid entertainment we were regaled with Lichfield ale which had a peculiar appropriated value. Sir Joshua and Dr. Burney and I drank cordially of it to Dr. Johnson's health, and though he would not join us he as cordially answered 'Gentlemen I wish you all as well as you do me.' (MS 829)

This cordial atmosphere prevails in the face of several potentially divisive topics. When the conversation turns to Thomas Hollis, a radical and irreligious democrat, Johnson's usual anxieties, hostilities, and dogmatisms are suspended. He moderates Elizabeth Carter's condemnation of Hollis's atheism, and even indulges in genial wordplay:

> *Mrs Carter* . . . I doubt he was an Atheist. *Johnson* [(smiling) *del*] I dont know that. He might perhaps have become one if he had had time to ripen ∧(smiling)∧ He might have *exuberated* into an Atheist. (MS 830)

The same amused tolerance governs his commentary on Hugh Blair's sermons:

> Though the dog is a Scotchman and a presbyterian and every thing he should not be, I was the first to praise them. Such was my candour ∧(smiling)∧ *Mrs Boscawen.* Such his great merit to get the better of all [this>] your prejudices. *Johnson.* Why Madam ∧ let us compound the matter. Let us ascribe it to∧ my candour and his merit. (MS 830)

In both his comments on Hollis and on Blair, Johnson relaxes into something that approaches self-parody: the move from 'ripen' to 'exuberate' mocks his penchant for polysyllabic Latinate diction, and the 'compounding' his Ramblerian taste for doublets.

Yet the schoolmaster, however benign he may be, is always on duty: later in the conversation, when 'somebody' (a daring or a forgetful 'somebody') declares that 'the Life of a mere literary man could not be very entertaining', Johnson is swift to correct:

But it certainly may. This is a remark which has been made and repeated without justice. Why should the life of a literary man be less entertaining than the life of any other man. Are there not as interesting varieties in such a life? As a literary life it may be very entertaining. (MS 831)

Absent from this rejoinder is any direct reference to Johnson's *Lives of the Poets* (the second instalment of which was about to appear). Yet Boswell works hard to make it tactfully clear how to construe Johnson's corrective. As his handling of the notes attests, he invites us to understand how the speech contributes to the scene while pointing beyond it: first we register the fact of Johnson's social self-command; then we go on to apply his remarks both to the *Lives* and to the *Life*. In their separate but complementary ways, Boswell suggests, both are brimming with 'interesting varieties'.

In the manuscript the gathering at Mrs Garrick's ends with a serio-comic reassertion of the authority that Johnson had been content to suspend, mute, and even parody. The tone of this final episode depends in large part on the stage directions that Boswell adds as he shapes the scene. The episode begins when Johnson tells the company of the printer's devil who married John Campbell.

(Then looking very serious and very earnest). And she did not disgrace him. The Woman had a bottom of good sense. The word *bottom* thus introduced was so ludicrous [in contrast to>] when contrasted with his gravity, that most of us could not forbear tittering and laughing, though I recollect that the Bishop of Kilaloe kept his countenance with perfect steadiness, [and>] while Miss Hannah More slyly hid her face behind a Lady's back who sat on the same settee with her. (MS 831–2)

The version in Boswell's notes supplies a minimum of interpretation:

He . . . cried, 'Where's the merriment?' Then, I believe wilfully, choosing a still more ludicrous word, and looking awful to show his power of restraint over us, he added, 'I say the woman was *fundamentally* sensible'—as if he had said, 'Hear this and laugh if you dare.' We were all close.[21]

The manuscript account, by contrast, attends closely to motivation and reception—to what is happening inside Johnson and around him:

His pride could not bear that any expression of his should excite ridicule when he did not intend it [ₐbut meant to be seriousₐ *del*]. He therefore resolved to assume and exercise despotick power, [looked>] glanced sternly [arround/round upon us>] arround and [called out>] asked in a strong tone 'Where's the merriment?' Then collecting himself, and looking awful to make us feel how he could impose restraint, and as it were searching his mind for a still more ludicrous word he slowly pronounced 'I say the *Woman* was *fundamentally* sensible' as if he had said hear this now and laugh if you dare. We all sat [in full composure>] composed as at a funeral. (MS 832)

These telling adjustments continue into the stage of proof: having chosen 'asked' in preference to 'called out' ('He . . . asked in a strong tone'), Boswell reverts to 'called out' as a way of dramatizing Johnson's vehement response. The final comparison ('as at a funeral') is a stroke of genius, for it ends the entire scene on the note of serious comedy with which it had begun. From start to finish, Boswell succeeds in holding opposites in delicate suspension: the grave and the ludicrous, the profound and the playful, the lively and the mournful. His labour of love is far from being lost.

Reporting to Edmond Malone on his progress with 'the first

---

[21] *Laird of Auchinleck*, ed. Reed and Pottle, 328–9 (20 Apr. 1781).

draught', Boswell noted that 'the Conversation with the King is to be formed into a complete scene out of the various minutes'.[22] Though this royal 'interview' testifies eloquently to Boswell's powers of selection and synthesis, no 'scene' in the *Life* is more 'complete' than the account of Johnson's first meeting with John Wilkes. Here Boswell contrives a perfect fit between the arts of social management that create the encounter and the arts of biographical management that do it full justice. In this instance, the original notes, which are quite cryptic, generate the narrative in the manuscript, which Boswell then revised several times over. The physical evidence suggests that, at an early stage of revision, Boswell detached the relevant leaves and circulated them among his friends, Wilkes perhaps among them: the leaves are folded and docketed on the outside 'First Conversation Between Dr. Johnson and Mr. Wilkes, 1776'. Below this docket is a note: 'It is prefaced in the book with a full Account of the *negociation* by which I led Johnson to affirm that meeting Mr. Wilkes would be nothing to him (affecting perfect ease of manners) so that when I brought them together he was *obliged* not to find fa<ult.>' (MS 607). This evidence helps to confer upon the Wilkes–Dilly episode the status of a highly polished, semi-autonomous artefact—a display piece that would function, like the Chesterfield letter, to epitomize and advertise the riches of the biography as a whole.

Boswell's notes, his cake of 'portable soup', preserve the core of the dialogue but little in the way of vivid or circumstantial detail.[23] When he transmutes these dehydrated pellets into biographical broth, he translates theatrical metaphor into structural

---

[22] Baker, 360 (17 Nov. 1788).

[23] 'I have thought my notes like portable soup, of which a little bit by being dissolved in water will make a good large dish' ('On Diaries', in *The Hypochondriack*, ed. Margery Bailey (Stanford, Calif.: Stanford Univ. Press, 1928)), 259.

practice more fully than anywhere else in the *Life*. The result is a miniature play, complete with prologue, rising action, blocking action, climax, and epilogue.[24]

The prologue emphasizes the difficulty of Boswell's self-appointed enterprise: 'to bring . . . together' men 'more different' than could be imagined. The two key verbs are 'negotiate' and 'manage'. Boswell tells Edward Dilly, his prospective host, 'if you'll let me negotiate for you I will be answerable that all shall go well.' Yet 'how to manage' this negotiation is 'a nice and difficult [question/matter>] matter' (MS 592–3). Boswell emphasizes the difficulty of the undertaking by describing Johnson and Wilkes as aggressive enemies locked in combat:

> They had even attacked [one another/each other>] one another [keenly/violently>] keenly in [their writings/print>] their writings; yet I lived in [very good habits>] habits of friendship with both, [and their arrows were shot over my head and by/past my sides but never through me *del*] (MS 592)

The version that Boswell settled on in proof tones down the violence of this image: 'They had even attacked one another with some asperity in their writings; yet I lived in habits of friendship with both.' It thereby diminishes the resonance of the phrase 'bond of union', with which Boswell marks the reconciliation of the two antagonists.

The playlet's blocking action begins when Boswell discovers on the afternoon of the dinner that Johnson has completely forgotten (or says that he has forgotten) the engagement at Dilly's. The first edition reads, 'I found him buffeting his books, as upon

---

[24] See Sven Eric Molin, 'Boswell's Account of the Johnson–Wilkes Meeting', *SEL* 3 (1963), 307–22. Molin's attempt to diagram the episode as a five-act neo-classical drama is overly schematic, but his underlying insight is fully supported by close study of the manuscripts: 'Boswell so clearly manages the whole and the transitions between the parts that . . . he could hardly have been unconscious of what Dryden calls the "design"' (ibid. 315).

a former occasion, covered with dust, and making no preparation for going abroad.' The celebrated verb 'buffeting' poses
a special challenge to editor and critic alike, for it emerges
from an unconscious collaboration between author and compositor. Boswell's original choice was 'battling with'—a choice
that derives from his journal entry for 3 April 1776:

> I called on Dr. Johnson; found him putting his books in order. He had
> gloves on, and was all dusty. He was quite in the character which Dr.
> Boswell drew of him: 'A robust genius! born to grapple with whole
> libraries!'[25]

As he revised his first draft, Boswell changed 'battling with'
to 'bustling among' (Fig. 7). However, the compositor misread
'bustling among' as 'buffeting among'. Because Boswell did not
read proof against printer's copy, he did not catch the error, and
settled for deleting 'among'. The result is an editorial crux that
might well occasion a latter-day grappling/battling/buffeting,
as Johnsonian upholders of an author's first intentions contend
with Wilkite proponents of a 'socialized' text.[26]

The blocking action continues when Johnson refuses to go to
Dilly's unless Anna Williams can be persuaded to release him.
The first draft captures the full measure of Boswell's frustration:
'Here was a sad dilemma. . . . He stood in some degree of awe of
Mrs. Williams and if she should be obstinate he would not stir'
(MS 596). In order to emphasize that Johnson was governed not
by female caprice but by his own code of courtesy, Boswell then
makes a significant alteration: 'He had accustomed himself to
shew Mrs. Williams such a degree of humane attention as sometimes imposed some restraint upon him, and I knew that if she
should be obstinate he would not stir.'

---

[25] *Ominous Years*, 310.

[26] Is a 'bond of union' possible? I myself prefer to live 'in habits of friendship
with both'.

This phase of the playlet makes especially effective use of Boswell's theatrical paradigm. Out of the briefest of notes, 'She peevish', he creates a scene of social seduction that owes its dynamics to Restoration comedy. By inviting us to imagine first the blind poet and then the Great Cham as objects of desire, Boswell narrowly skirts the grotesque. But his pair of implied comparisons—of Mrs Williams to an ingénue who 'softened to my solicitations', and of Johnson to an heiress who is spirited off to Gretna Green—brilliantly serves the purpose of making us 'live o'er each scene'. At the same time, Boswell signals his structural debt to neoclassical drama by heightening an allusion to *Cato*. When he has persuaded Mrs Williams to release Dr Johnson, Boswell returns to the study and finds him, in the original reading, 'indifferent in his choice, Dilly's or home' (MS 597). The quotation floats to the surface when the phrase becomes 'indifferent in his choice to go or stay'—a direct parallel to Addison's line, 'indiff'rent in his choice to sleep or die'.[27]

Boswell's notes suggest that the conversation at Dilly's did not progress in a sustained arc, but moved instead by fits and starts. As he expands the notes, Boswell repositions blocks of dialogue, creating a growing sense of cordiality as Johnson and Wilkes discover common ground. Perhaps the single most striking moment in the entire *Life* occurs when they turn the tables on their tormentor:

I claimed a superiority for Scotland over England in one respect, that no man can be arrested there for a debt . . . [unless] his creditor should swear that he is . . . *in meditatione fugae*. WILKES. 'That, I should think, may be safely sworn of all the Scotch nation.' JOHNSON. (to Mr. Wilkes) 'You must know, Sir, I lately took my friend Boswell and shewed him genuine civilised life in an English provincial town. I turned him loose

---

[27] Addison, *Cato* v. i. 40, in *Eighteenth-Century Plays*, introd. Ricardo Quintana (New York: Modern Library, 1952), 51.

at Lichfield, my native city, that he might see for once real civility: for you know he lives among savages in Scotland, and among rakes in London.' WILKES. 'Except when he is with grave, sober, decent people like you and me.' JOHNSON. (smiling) 'And we ashamed of him.' (*Life* iii. 77)

Boswell fashions this climax, which feels inevitable in its every nuance, out of inchoate materials:

Talk of swearing a debt. I mentioned not in Scotland but in meditat fugae. *Wilkes* Then it may be of all the Scotch. Arch Duke of Argyll quite a household God, the best Landlord—had got into his Anecdotage. *Johns* I took Bo to see civilised life in an english provinc town. I turned him loose at Litchfield to see civility for you know he lives among savages at home and among rakes in London. *Wilkes* Except when he is with sober people like you and me. *Johns* (laughing) And we ashamed of him. *Wilkes* Bos you have kept a great deal of bad company.

Boswell's first decision is to cut the reference to the Duke of Argyll, so that Wilkes's 'That I think' becomes more clearly what might be described as a feeder line. He then adds to Johnson's speech the stage direction 'To Mr. Wilkes', the introductory 'You must know, Sir,' the adjectives 'genuine' and 'real', and the epithet 'my native city'. Taken together, these changes make of the speech a pointed challenge to Wilkes and a sly criticism of Boswell; they also inject a faint but unmistakable note of self-directed irony, as Johnson plays up the status of Lichfield as a school for rakish savages and savage rakes.

Boswell's additions continue with the adjectives 'grave' and 'sober': these make Wilkes's response an antiphonal exercise in recognition and deflection. The stage direction 'laughing' disappears at first but resurfaces as 'smiling'—a sign that Boswell has decided to retain a tonal marker but to inflect it as subtly as possible. Finally, he cuts Wilkes's blunt criticism ('you have kept a great deal of bad company'), which undercuts the impact of the sly collaboration between Johnson and Wilkes.

The dramatic structure of the whole is completed by the addition, at a later stage of revision, of a one-sentence epilogue: 'Mr. Burke gave me much credit for this successful *negociation* and pleasantly said that there was nothing to equal it in the whole history of the *Corps Diplomatique*' (MS 606). This verdict reintroduces the idea of negotiation and crowns Boswell's achievement with the accolade of a brilliant (and highly theatrical) politician.

When he comes to describe the second meeting between Johnson and Wilkes, Boswell designs a pendant to his playlet.[28] The introduction leaves no doubt that the episodes are meant to be viewed as a pair: 'On tuesday eighth May I had the pleasure of again dining with him and Mr. Wilkes, at Mr. Dilly's. No *Negociation* was now required to bring them together for Johnson was so well satisfied with the former interview that he was very glad to meet Mr. Wilkes again' (MS 833–4). Like the previous conversation, morever, this one was docketed, detached, and vetted by friends. This time there can be no doubt that Wilkes was one of the readers, for all the most significant changes consist of supplements to his speeches. Boswell retains firm control of the episode, however, by framing the conversation with care. At the beginning he adds a remark by Pasquale Paoli that emphasizes the dramatic and even the allegorical dimensions of the encounter: Wilkes, we are told, 'was this day seated between [Dr. Johnson and Dr. Beattie>] Dr. Beattie and Dr. Johnson ∧(between Truth and Reason as General Paoli said when I told him of it)∧' (MS 834). At the end of the conversation he supplies a coda, which invites the reader to contemplate Wilkes and Johnson as if they were on stage:

---

[28] No notes or journal entries relating to this episode have been recovered. See *Laird of Auchinleck*, ed. Reed and Pottle, 348.

I [myself *del*] left the room for a little while. When I returned I was
struck with observing Dr. Samuel Johnson and John Wilkes Esq.
literally *tete á tete*; for they were [sitting close with their>] reclined
upon their chairs with their heads leaning almost close to each other,
and talking earnestly in a kind of confidential whisper of the personal
quarrel between George the Second and the King of Prussia. (MS
838–9)

Having invited us to watch the two men 'talking earnestly',
Boswell creates a freeze-frame effect that reinvokes Paoli's allegorical comparison:

Such a [perfect easy sociality>] [scene of perfect easy social inter-
course>] scene of perfectly easy sociality between two such opponents
in the war of political controversy as ∧that which∧ I now beheld, would
have been [a very good>] [a happy>] an excellent subject for a picture.
∧It presented to my mind the happy days which are foretold in scrip-
ture, when the Lion shall lye down with the Kid.∧ (MS 839)

As he drafts and redrafts this passage, Boswell finds ways of
concluding both this conversation and its predecessor. The
final tableau restages the climax of the playlet, when the two
arch-antagonists first find themselves 'tête-à-tête'. The martial
metaphor brings back the themes of 'negotiation' and 'union'.
Finally, in its mock-epic tone Boswell's reference to the peace-
able kingdom gestures toward Burke's diplomatic compliment.
For a second time the curtain is rung down with a graceful yet
emphatic epilogue.[29]

   Theatricality, in sum, pervades every aspect of the biography's
scenic construction. Boswell's multiple roles in the *Life* correlate
to his multiple models: the epic, the saint's life, the portrait,
the play, the epistolarium. In this lecture we have been considering his operations as playwright, who creates conversational
performance-pieces of many genres and sizes. What is common

---

[29] Cf. ibid. 348–51 (8 May 1781).

to all these operations is the goal of transparency. As William C. Dowling observes, 'The illusion as we encounter it throughout the biographical story is that the *Life* includes its imaginary audience in the conversation scenes, that the audience is present whenever Johnson speaks in just the same sense as Boswell is present, or Goldsmith, or any other member of that numerous company that surrounds Johnson in the typical scene in which he holds forth on the topic of the moment.'[30] To make us fully present Boswell tries to make himself, *as biographical craftsman,* fully absent. That is the danger of our analytic enterprise: attending to technique, we run the risk of obscuring or even dispelling the dramatic illusion of presence. It is a price worth paying, however, if it allows the playwright to take a long-postponed bow.

---

[30] William C. Dowling, *Language and Logos in Boswell's* Life of Johnson (Princeton: Princeton Univ. Press, 1981), 100–1.

4

Transmitting Johnson

In the autumn of 1790, Frances Burney, then serving as second keeper of the robes to Queen Charlotte, finds herself re-enacting the role of one of her fictional heroines. Like the well-named Evelina Anville, upon whom shamelessly aggressive males are forever hammering, Burney is trapped in a crowded public space by an importunate suitor. In this instance the setting is Windsor Castle and the suitor is James Boswell, who is seeking not sexual but literary favours. First Boswell embarrasses Burney by declaring, in the midst of 'a multitude', that she must resign her position at Court. Next, he commands her to contribute to his biography:

'Yes, madam; you must give me some of your choice little notes of the Doctor's; we have seen him long enough upon stilts; I want to show him in a new light. . . . I want to show him as gay Sam, agreeable Sam, pleasant Sam: so you must help me with some of his beautiful billets to yourself.'[1]

Burney's repeated refusals only intensify Boswell's pleas. Directly in front of the Queen's Lodge, 'with crowds passing and repassing', he pulls 'a proof sheet out of his pocket' and insists upon reading her a passage. What Boswell chooses as an example of his work-in-progress, an example he hopes will overcome Burney's scruples, is a letter from Johnson. 'He read it', Burney reluctantly admits, 'in strong imitation of the Doctor's manner, very well, and not caricature.' But the momentary spell is broken when she sees the royal family approaching and hurries away

---

[1] *Diary and Letters of Madame d'Arblay*, ed. Charlotte Barrett, rev. Austin Dobson, 6 vols. (London: Henry Colburn, 1904–5), iv. 432–3.

in distress. Recounting the incident to her sister Susan, Burney declares that nothing will convince her 'to print private letters, even of a man so justly celebrated, when addressed to myself'. This memorable vignette tells us as much about Boswell as it does about Burney. Printing 'private letters' is for her a violation, for him a vindication—a vindication of his protagonist and a vindication of his biographical method. As Boswell assures other potential contributors, only Johnson's letters will 'illustrate' his protagonist's many facets and thereby 'do credit . . . to his heart'.[2]

Boswell intends, in short, to 'shew us the *Man*', a man who is not only Doctor Johnson 'upon stilts' but also 'gay Sam, agreeable Sam, pleasant Sam'.[3] But showing depends upon telling. Central to the encounter at Windsor is Boswell's attempt to convince Burney by reading one of Johnson's letters out loud— 'very well, and not caricature'. Burney's phrase, 'not caricature', registers Boswell's gift for ventriloquizing Johnson, for preserving and transmitting His Master's Voice. By applying the word 'caricature' to an oral performance of an epistolary text, she collaborates unwittingly with Boswell in allying the visual with the verbal. Rushed and truncated it may have been, but his performance of the Doctor's matter 'in strong imitation of the Doctor's manner' transmits to her a speaking likeness.

Epistolary fiction in the hands of a Samuel Richardson wins admiration and even reverence; epistolary biography in the hands of a James Boswell earns condescension and even contempt. 'It is a truth universally acknowledged' by the School of Greene that Boswell depended upon Johnson's letters to vitalize his feeble rhetoric and to plug gaping holes in his primary

---

[2] See Boswell's letters to J. B. Pearson, 7 Apr. 1785, and Sarah Adams, 5 May 1786 (Waingrow, 76, 123).

[3] Boswell to W. J. Temple, 24–5 Feb. 1788 (ibid. 208).

sources. According to this view, Boswell inserted letters mechanically by date, thereby producing an awkward amalgam of anthology and chronicle. Even Greene's arch-antagonist, Frederick Pottle *Boswellianissimus*, tends to consider the letters more of a liability than a strength. In order to maintain his grip on the reins, Pottle believes, Boswell 'counted on the conversations to dominate and control the letters, and he did not trust in vain'.[4] For Greene, the profusion of letters clutters and distracts; for Pottle, it creates problems of authority that must be counteracted by rigorous subjugation.

Such pejorative views originate in Boswell's inability or unwillingness to do justice to his own designs. As we have seen in other contexts, the biographer leads readers to devalue his achievement by attributing it to industry rather than art. On those infrequent occasions, for example, when he talks explicitly about his use of letters, he consistently uses the verbs 'insert' or 'interweave' and the nouns 'collection' or 'compendium'.[5] In this same vein, Boswell gives the reader an emphatic (and emphatically misleading) view of his enterprise when he pays tribute at the beginning of the *Life* to William Mason, a true drudge and a false biographer:

Instead of melting down my materials into one mass, and constantly speaking in my own person . . . I have resolved to adopt and enlarge upon the excellent plan of Mr. Mason, in his Memoirs of Gray. Wherever narrative is necessary to explain, connect, and supply, I furnish it to the best of my abilities; but in the chronological series of Johnson's life, which I trace as distinctly as I can, year by year, I produce,

---

[4] Frederick A. Pottle, '*The* Life of Johnson: *Art and Authenticity*', in James L. Clifford (ed.), *Twentieth-Century Interpretations of Boswell's* Life of Johnson (Englewood Cliffs, NJ: Prentice-Hall, 1970), 72.

[5] See, for example, the letters to William Bowles, 27 Feb. 1786, and to James Beattie, 30 Oct. 1787 (Waingrow, 109–10, 188).

wherever it is in my power, his own minutes, letters, or conversation. (*Life* i. 29)

Caveat lector: though Boswell singles it out for praise and emulation, William Mason's *Memoirs of the Life and Writings of Mr Gray* (1775) deserves nothing more than the modest label 'compendium', if it deserves that. As Frank Brady explains, 'William Mason's *Gray* was unusual in being made up of a long series of the subject's letters—which Mason, we now know, rephrased, bowdlerized, truncated, spliced together, and misdated—linked by a trickle of mealy-mouthed explanation.'[6] Yet from Boswell's perspective the 'excellent plan' of these epistolary *Memoirs*, which allows the reader direct access to the subject, suggests ways in which he can make his biography '*more* of a *Life* than any Work that has ever yet appeared'.[7]

Though Boswell may have said that he merely 'compiled' his biography, the manuscript contradicts his testimony: it reveals that he *composed* it.[8] I propose to oust 'compile' in favour of 'compose' because 'compose' suggests both the shaping of a picture space and the creation of a musical score. That Boswell himself thought simultaneously in terms of the aural and the pictorial is revealed by a small but significant choice. As he revises the narrative for 1781, Boswell introduces three letters from Warren Hastings by observing: 'The last of these letters thus graciously put into my hands and which has already appeared in publick belongs to this year; but I shall previously insert the two first in the order of their dates. They altogether form a grand groupe

---

    [6] Brady, 427–8.

    [7] Boswell to W. J. Temple, 24–5 Feb. 1788 (Waingrow, 208).

    [8] Compare Marshall Waingrow's observation: 'The *Life* is less a compilation—one of Boswell's favourite and most misleading descriptions of the work—than it is a composition, in the full literary sense of that word' (ibid. p. xxxiii).

in my Biographical [Tablature/Picture>] Picture.'[9] In the eighteenth century, 'tablature' meant both 'musical notation' and 'painting'. Boswell's first choice creates an ambiguity that he decides to eliminate by choosing 'Picture'; the advantage of 'Picture' is that it correlates exactly to 'grand groupe'. Nonetheless, the deleted alternative gives us insight into Boswell's understanding of his compositional craft.

At the same time that he chose 'Picture' over 'Tablature', Boswell wrote to Malone, announcing his decision to incorporate not only the three letters in question but also a letter from Hastings to Boswell: 'I have received . . . Johnson's letters to Mr. Hastings—three in all—one of them long and admirable; but what sets the diamonds in pure gold of Ophir is a letter from Mr. Hastings to me illustrating them and their Writer.'[10] Just as he judges that Hastings's letter forms an ideal setting for the three Johnsonian jewels, so Boswell nestles other such jewels in mounts of his own devising. The art of transmitting Johnson consists in part of selecting and editing the letters themselves—a process that the manuscript does little to document.[11] What are preserved in abundance, however, are the traces of Boswell as goldsmith, who chooses *where* to 'set' the letters (in the sense of 'position') and *how* to 'set' them (in the sense of 'surround'). It is to these traces that we now turn our attention.

---

[9] Paper Apart, Gen Mss 89, Box 56, Folder 1189 (cf. *Life* iv. 67).

[10] Baker, 376.

[11] Moreover, Boswell's activities as collector-editor have been well studied by R. W. Chapman and Marshall Waingrow: see *The Letters of Samuel Johnson*, ed. Chapman (Oxford: Clarendon Press, 1952), iii. 305–9 and Waingrow, pp. xxviii–xliii.

Epistolary Frames

'Take it in': this directive to the compositor appears most frequently in connection with Papers Apart that consist of or incorporate letters. It cannot be denied that Boswell's decisions to 'take in' are often governed by the rudimentary laws of chronology. Yet many leaves of the manuscript suggest that Boswell cared to dispose as well as interpose. His disposition of epistolary materials falls into two categories: framing (or reframing) and positioning (or repositioning).

The framing of letters takes various forms. On occasion, Boswell will decide that his reasons for including a given letter need to be spelled out; in order to explain his choice, he will append a footnote that seeks to interpret the letter as well. A plangent letter from Johnson to Baretti, for example, acquires a note in proof: 'This is a very just account of the relief which London affords to melancholy minds' (*Life MS* i. 257 n. 7). Boswell takes pains with the phrasing of this note, experimenting with 'exquisite' and 'admirable' before settling on 'just', and changing 'minds of sensibility' to 'melancholy minds'. The implication is twofold: Johnson is to be admired for vigorously combating his depression; the biographer speaks out of shared experience. Through such glosses, Boswell bolsters his own authority and fits specific letters into a consistent interpretation of his hero's experience.

More powerful because more pervasive are the introductions, bridge passages, and conclusions that Boswell creates for the main text. When an important correspondent enters the *Life*, Boswell usually supplies both biographical information and commentary that works to infiltrate the ensuing letters. Nowhere does such commentary matter more than in the prelude to the Johnson–Boswell correspondence:

Utrecht having at first appeared very dull to me after the animated
scenes of London, my spirits were [sadly>] grievously affected; and
I [first *del*] wrote ∧/to/ Johnson∧ a plaintive and desponding letter
[which he treated with a cold and stern neglect>] to which he paid
no regard. Afterwards when I [was in a better frame>] [was in a
firmer frame>] [had acquired/attained to a firmer tone of mind>] had
acquired a firmer tone of mind, I wrote him a second letter expressing
much anxiety to hear from him; and then came the following Epistle
which was of important service to me, and I trust will be so also to many
[more>] others. (*Life MS* i. 332–3)

As he revises, Boswell struggles for control of tone, just as he
has struggled at Utrecht for 'a firmer tone of mind'. He seeks to
position us both inside and outside the scene—to elicit sympathy
for his young, 'desponding' self but also to present Johnson as
a disciplinarian whose severity produces beneficial results. The
single most striking change, the transformation of 'which he
treated with a cold and stern neglect' into 'to which he paid no
regard', erases any suggestion that Boswell continues to resent
his subject's behaviour. More than that: it aligns the first epistolary exchange with the first conversational exchange, in which
devastating reproof had given way to bracing generosity. Finally,
the biographer who opens his work by quoting *Rambler* No. 60
generalizes here, in best Johnsonian fashion, from the particulars of the incident: 'then came the following Epistle which was
of important service to me, and I trust will be so also to many
[more>] others.' Implicit in this declaration is the belief that the
reader can and should find most of Johnson's letters 'of important service'.

In a similar vein the drafts of Boswell's introduction to the
Thomas Warton letters show him attentive to nuances of tone
and issues of authority. Warton had sent Boswell a notebook that
included copies of Johnson's letters as well as explanatory notes.

Boswell's first impulse is to acknowledge Warton's assistance in effusive terms and to minimize his own role:

He this year found ∧an interval of∧ leisure to make an excursion to Oxford, for the purpose of [consultation of the>] consulting the Libraries there. Of this and of many interesting circumstances concerning him [in the years 1754 and 1755 a part/an important part>] during a part of his life when he conversed but little with the World I am enabled to give [an entertaining>] a particular account by the [∧very∧ *del*] liberal [kindness>] communications of the Reverend Mr. Thomas Warton who [most obligingly>] has obligingly [sent me a collection/ number of letters from him illustrated with notes by Mr. Warton>] furnished me with several of our common friend's letters which he has illustrated with notes. [These I shall insert in their order>] These I shall insert in their proper places. (*Life MS* i. 195)

Considered as a whole, Boswell's revisions downplay Warton's gesture while decorously acknowledging his contribution, gently cultivating the reader's interest, and quietly stressing the biographer's role. Boswell settles on neutral terms: 'a part of his life' instead of 'an important part of his life', 'a particular account' instead of 'an entertaining account'. He dilutes the compliments to Warton and discards the initial alternatives, 'a collection' and 'a number', in favour of 'several'; in fact, there were eighteen letters in all. In addition, he subtly but significantly reshapes the final sentence: to change 'insert in their order' to 'insert in their proper places' is to keep the biographer's prerogative and the biographer's criteria firmly to the fore.

In his introduction to the Warton letters, Boswell uses the verb 'illustrate' to mean 'explain, clear, elucidate'. More often than not, however, he sets about 'illustrating' Johnson in the first two senses of the word: 'to brighten with light', 'to brighten with honour'.[12] 'To brighten with honour' is precisely Boswell's

---

[12] These definitions are taken from Johnson's *Dictionary*, 4th edn. (1773).

purpose in including a pair of letters within the narrative for 1777. The manuscript reveals that the original plan called for just one, a letter to the clergyman William Vyse that seeks Vyse's support for an impoverished descendant of Hugo Grotius. Boswell then decided to add a second letter on the same topic, this one to Bennet Langton. In this instance the revisions continued beyond the manuscript into first proof; the presence of Malone's hand in the manuscript indicates that he played a part as well.

Boswell structures his introduction as if it were a paragraph from the *Rambler* or the *Idler*. A sweeping generalization narrows in graded stages to a set of specific examples:

His benevolence [to/towards] to the unfortunate was I am confident as steady and active as that of any [man who ever existed>] of those eminent persons who have been most distinguished for it. Innumerable instances of it I have no doubt will be forever concealed from mortal [inquiry>] research. We may however judge from the many and very various specimens which happened to be discovered. One in the course of this summer ∧he wrote to Mr. Langton. Another∧ [13] is remarkable from the name and connection of its object and has been [kindly/obligingly>] obligingly communicated to me by the Reverend Dr. Vyse Rector of Lambeth. (MS 619) [14]

As the manuscript attests, Boswell eliminated the hyperbolic reference to 'any man who ever existed'. By changing 'inquiry' to 'research' in the second sentence, he signals that he is speaking out of his own experience as a biographer who 'spared no pains in obtaining materials concerning' Johnson (*Life* i. 26). By the time of second proof, however, he had made changes that undercut his first set of revisions and markedly altered the tone of the whole. In the first sentence, 'any of those eminent persons

[13] This addition ('he wrote to Mr. Langton. Another') is in the hand of Malone.

[14] MS 619: Houghton Library, Harvard University.

who have been most distinguished for it [benevolence]' gives
way to the more sonorous, more didactic 'any of those who have
been eminently distinguished for that virtue'. In the second sentence, the language turns spiritual and the emphasis on human
enquiry disappears—witness the conversion of 'instances' into
'proofs', 'mortal research' into 'mortal eyes'. In line with these
changes, the third sentence, which centres on the word 'specimens', loses its sharp focus: 'We may, however, form some
judgement of it, from the many and very various instances
which have been discovered.' By substituting 'instances' for
'specimens', Boswell has diminished the materiality of the letters—their tangible, legible identity as witnesses to Johnson's
benevolence. The result is to elide the deed with the documentation of that deed.

Letters that 'illustrate' become more and more important in
the final stages of the biography, as Johnson's health declines and
Boswell's narrative begins to centre on a struggle that is at once
physical, intellectual, and spiritual. Because his public literary
career was essentially over, and the great evenings of conversation a thing of the past, letters function as vital proofs of *vivida vis*,
the defining characteristic Boswell singles out in the final Character. The biographer's source material narrows in direct proportion to his subject's disabilities, a fact that becomes clear if we
take note of the deleted clause in the introduction to the narrative for 1782: 'In 1782 his complaints increased and the history
of his life for this year [so far as I have been able to collect it *del*]
is little more than a mournful recital of the variations of his ill-
ness, in the midst of which however it will appear from his letters
that the powers of his mind were in no degree impaired' (MSS
857–8).

Not only the substance of these sickbed letters but their style
as well testifies to Johnson's resilience:

[During>] Notwithstanding his afflicted state of body and mind this year, the following correspondence affords a proof not only of his benevolence and conscientious readiness to relieve [even an unknown good man>] a good man from errour but by his clothing one of the sentiments in his Rambler in different language, ∧not inferiour to that of the original∧ shews his [admirable>] [singular>] extraordinary command of clear and forcible expression.

In order to drive home his central theme, *mens sana in corpore aegro*, Boswell adds a clause ('not inferiour to that of the original') that emphasizes Johnson's undiminished powers as a writer; moreover, he reinforces his comparison to the *Rambler* by settling carefully on an adjective, 'extraordinary', that will combine with the noun 'command' to convey the strongest possible impression of Johnson's goodness, his courage, and his genius.

At times Boswell's introductions draw the reader into his biographical workshop, where we learn about his sources and listen to him making decisions about what to include and how to include it. Such framing commentary is especially effective when it accompanies extracts rather than entire letters:

I have in my possession several more letters from him to Mr. Cruickshank, and also to [the very ingenious *del*] Dr. Mudge at Plymouth which it would be improper to insert as they are filled with unpleasing technical details. I shall however [excerpt>] extract from his letters to Dr. Mudge [to whom he says 'I trust much to your judgement' *del*] such passages as [will *del*] shew either a felicity of expression, or the undaunted state of his mind. (MS 915–16)

Unlike the introductions we have just been considering, this passage offers us two distinct possibilities: we can approach the letters as human or as literary documents. Boswell thereby forestalls any impulse to question the worth of his selection: if we find a given text substandard on stylistic grounds, we are silenced by its 'admirable' or 'singular' content.

Epistolary Mosaics

Thus far we have been attending to the ways in which Boswell frames or reframes letters by providing explicit commentary. The manuscript of the *Life* also reveals the care that went into positioning letters so as to gloss, punctuate, or advance the narrative. With these goals in mind, Boswell adopts three basic tactics. First, he changes the disposition of letters without altering the selection of letters. Second, he alters both disposition and selection; quite often, the one necessitates the other. Third, he creates and perfects an epistolary sequence, a sequence that can include as many as ten to fifteen letters. Let us consider each of these tactics in turn.

To watch Boswell moving letters from place to place is to admire his sense of pace and proportion. At the beginning of the narrative for 1766, he distils two crisp sentences out of a rambling lament for Johnson's deficiencies as a correspondent:

Both in 1764 and 1765 it [would>] should seem [that his habitual 'loathing to write'/constitutional unwillingness to write prevailed in a most remarkable degree. Though I wrote to him frequently in the course of these years, while I was upon my travels I did not receive a single letter in return yet he was pleased with a letter which I wrote to him from the Tomb of Melancthon>] [that his habitual 'loathing to write'/ constitutional unwillingness to write prevailed in a most remarkable degree. I have discovered no letter except one to Reynolds and though I wrote to him frequently in the course of these two years while I was upon my travels but did not receive a single letter in return he was afterwards pleased with a letter which I wrote to him from the Tomb of Melancthon>] that he was so busily employed with his edition of Shakspeare as to have had [no leisure for any other literary exertion or even indeed/and indeed little even for>] little leisure for any other literary exertion or indeed even for private correspondence. I wrote to him frequently in the course of these two years while I was upon my travels but did not receive a single letter in return for which ∧it will appear that∧ he afterwards apologised. (*Life MS* ii. 1)

As it evolves, this passage moves away from speculation and complaint to inference and fact: during these years, Johnson was working on his *Shakespeare*, and his labours as an editor were the likely cause of his lapses as a letter-writer. A direction to the compositor, cued to 'Tomb of Melancthon', indicates that Boswell intended originally to include the letter he had written in Wittenberg. At a later stage he decides that this letter will serve better as a gloss upon one of Johnson's letters from 1777, in which Johnson thanks Boswell for sending him 'your two letters that had been kept so long in store' (*Life* iii. 122). This decision allows Boswell to include a document of which he is proud, but to relegate it to the margins and thereby to keep his protagonist sympathetically to the fore.

One of the points at which the distinction between biography and autobiography comes closest to blurring is the section devoted to the Auchinleck entail. At the beginning of 'Paper Apart E' ('E' for 'Entail'), Boswell labours to justify what might otherwise seem flagrantly tangential: this complex family dispute, he claims, elicited from Johnson a response that illustrates the unusual range and depth of his intellect. But Boswell faced a major rhetorical problem: the reader, like Mrs Bennet in *Pride and Prejudice*, might well react to the technicalities of the entail with uncomprehending dismay. On the other hand, the matter must be made clear if the acuity of Johnson's analysis is to make itself felt.

Boswell launches himself gingerly into the details of the case: 'That what he wrote upon the subject may be understood it is necessary to give a state of the question which I shall [endeavour to do with brevity and precision>] do as briefly as I can' (*Life*

MS ii. 177). How to achieve such 'brevity and precision'? Initially Boswell decides to tell his story through an array of letters, which will convey the principle at stake and the emotions it excites. These letters will be followed by an expository section devoted to legal and genealogical details. At a later stage, he concludes that the epistolary block should follow the expository section—that the letters require an explanatory preface. Though he may not succeed in animating the topic, or convincing us that it belongs in a biography of Johnson, he demonstrates yet again his skill at making the most of different kinds of evidence.

Boswell's second tactic as disposer of letters is to reconsider where they should be placed and how they should be represented. The possible consequences of moving a letter include both promotion and demotion: summaries can be upgraded to extracts, extracts to full texts; full texts can be downgraded and even eliminated. An example of promotion occurs early in the *Life*, during the account of Johnson's work on the *Gentleman's Magazine*, and of demotion during the summary of the Hebridean tour in 1773.

As he drafts his narrative of Johnson's early years in Grub Street, Boswell decides to summarize two letters to Cave, the first signed 'impransus' and the second recommending Alexander Macbean:

> In the Gentleman's Magazine for January 1785 there is a letter . . . which is remarkable in that it concludes yours *impransus* SAM JOHNSON; and it is no less remarkable that though in this state of want himself his benevolent heart was not insensible to the necessities of an humble labourer in literature; for the very next letter earnestly recommends 'the eldest Mr. Macbean' to be employed by Mr. Cave to compile a Military Dictionary. (*Life MS* i. 93)

As he revises, he decides to include a complete text of both these letters. Having taken that decision, he postpones the appearance of the letters so that they follow his description of the project to translate Sarpi's *History of the Council of Trent*; he also creates an emphatic link passage between the first letter and the second, a passage that will draw attention to Johnson's poverty and his generosity: '∧It is remarkable that Johnson's last quoted letter to Mr. Cave concludes with a fair confession that he had not a dinner, and it is no less remarkable that though in this state of want himself, his benevolent heart was not insensible to the necessities of an humble labourer as appears from the [following>] very next letter' (*Life MS* i. 95). Early in the writing of the *Life*, Boswell is already practising in tandem the arts of repositioning and reframing.

Not only do letters grow and multiply during the course of revision, they also dwindle and disappear. As Boswell reshapes his account of the Hebridean jaunt, he substitutes summary for excerpts in the epistolary sequence that explains the background. When he reconsiders how best to narrate the trip itself, he decides to eliminate letters entirely. This decision, which shrinks the narrative to a single terse paragraph, appears to have been motivated by two concerns. First, Boswell feared duplicating materials that had already appeared in his *Journal of a Tour to the Hebrides*. As he explains in a sentence that never made it into print: 'To embody [the story] here would render this publication/the present compilation too bulky; besides that it would justly be thought unbecoming in me to load a great many of my readers with the purchase of that/a Book/a Collection of which they are allready in possession' (*Life MS* ii. 118). The second probable reason for the disappearance of letters at this stage is Boswell's decision to combine details of the trip with an account of Johnson's *Journey to the Western Islands of Scotland*. We do in fact revisit the journey, but we do so as it was filtered through the *Journey*. As a consequence, Boswell preserves what

Paul Alkon has called the biography's 'unity of cultural place':
the action remains centred on London, and Johnson the traveller
is subordinated to Johnson the travel-writer.[15]

Thus far we have been attending to the ways in which Boswell
refines the placement (and along with the placement, the selection) of individual letters. But individual letters can also be
grouped together into an epistolary suite or sequence. Key
sections of the *Life* are in fact made up of such sequences, to
whose design Boswell devoted considerable care. In structural
terms they serve multiple purposes—none more important than
the launching or sustaining of the narrative for a particular year.
Let us investigate first the sequences that open 1772 and 1777,
and then turn our attention to the skilfully engineered span
that carries forward the account of Johnson's final visit to the
Midlands.

Boswell never allows us to forget the chronological structure
of the *Life*: not only does most of the narrative subdivide into
annual units, but the double temporal marker at the top of every
page (e.g. '1767, Aetat. 58') signposts both the hero's and the
reader's long journey. This structure poses at least one recurrent
challenge: since 'Year chases Year', how to avoid the wearying
impression that 'Decay pursues Decay'? How, in short, to begin
each narrative unit afresh? As Boswell creates the narrative for
1772, he decides first on an epistolary opening—an edited version of his letter to Johnson written from Edinburgh on 3 March.
This decision means that the story of 1772 would have begun
with a complaint of neglect: 'It is hard that I cannot prevail
on you to write to me oftener. But I am convinced that it is in
vain to expect from you a private correspondence with any reg-
ularity' (*Life* ii. 144). On reflection, Boswell decides to create a

---

[15] Paul K. Alkon, 'Boswellian Time', *Studies in Burke and his Time*, 14 (Spring
1973), 255.

more vibrant, affirmative opening. Accordingly, he inserts a pair of letters that tell an engaging anecdote: in conversation with Joseph Banks and Daniel Solander, Johnson has been asked to devise a motto for the goat that accompanied Captain Cook around the world; instead of a motto, he comes up with a Latin distich, which he sends to Banks via Joshua Reynolds. By starting off the year with these letters, Boswell emphasizes not passivity but reciprocity: 'In 1772 he was altogether quiescent as an Authour; but it will be found from the various evidences which I shall bring together, that his mind was acute lively and vigorous' (*Life MS* ii. 67). In order to emphasize the theme of mental vigour, he also moves a letter from Johnson to Bennet Langton (a letter that he thought at one point of placing directly after the letter about the goat) to the end of the opening sequence. These changes transform the opening of 1772: what was once querulous and repetitive is now witty and engaging. Moreover, the changes help to convince us that letters do indeed constitute 'various evidences' of Johnson's unflagging powers.

After quoting briefly from Johnson's diaries and prayers, Boswell begins the narrative for 1777 with a sequence of eight letters.[16] In the middle of this sequence he places the 'Proposals' for William Shaw's *Analysis of the Galic Language*, one of Johnson's many anonymous contributions to the work of others. By the time of revised proof, these 'Proposals' had been moved forward in the sequence, so that they fall in between Boswell's letters of 4 and 24 April. This shift in position has three effects. It preserves the antiphonal nature of the sequence by making Johnson's voice, speaking through the 'Proposals', respond to

---

[16] The order in the *Life MS* is as follows: Boswell to Johnson, 14 Feb.; Alexander Dick to Johnson, 17 Feb.; Johnson to Boswell, 18 Feb.; Boswell to Johnson, 24 Feb.; Johnson to Boswell, 11 Mar.; Shaw's 'Proposals'; Boswell to Johnson, 4 Apr.; Boswell to Johnson, 24 Apr.; Johnson to Boswell, 3 May (MS 617, Houghton Library).

Boswell's voice. It prepares for the 'Proposals' by introducing the topic in Boswell's letter of 4 April. And it separates the news of David Boswell's death, which comes in the letter of 4 April, from the mention of Henry Thrale's death in Johnson's letter of 24 April. Such effects suggest that Boswell was continuously alive to the epistolary sequence as a semi-autonomous unit, and that he cared for both thematic continuity and tonal variety within the sequence. His greatest achievement in this vein is the span of letters that stretches without a break from July to November 1784.

As we observed in the second chapter, Boswell arranges the penultimate section of the *Life* so that it reverses the movement with which the biography began. Our last sight of Johnson is Boswell's, the parting in London that 'impressed [him] with a foreboding of [their] long, long separation' (*Life* iv. 339). Thenceforth the fully incarnate hero recedes from view as he makes his final trip to the Midlands. Johnson manifests himself through his letters alone—and these letters are dominated by the topic of disease. The paradox is that, in being reminded continuously of Johnson the physical being, we are distanced from the physical. We participate in his struggle but only at an ever-increasing remove: a voice that speaks of the body comes to seem disembodied.

At the same time that he prepares this vanishing act, Boswell seeks to shape Johnson's 'various mass of correspondence' so that it will exhibit 'a genuine and noble specimen of vigour and vivacity of *mind* which neither age nor sickness could impair or diminish' (Paper Apart cued to MS 1001, my emphasis). Boswell's syntax, with its insistent use of doublets, works like the opening sentence of the biography: it imitates Johnson's style as a means of paying tribute to him. So too Boswell's selection and arrangement of Johnson's letters distils a linguistic essence that is also a human reality. As he fights his losing battle, Johnson struggles with and through language; Boswell's anthology aims to recapture that struggle as vividly as possible.

The final sequence consists of letters to thirteen correspondents. Through them Boswell creates the equivalent of a miniature epistolary novel, which refracts Johnson's experience prismatically. This tactic mirrors Johnson's own commitment to seeing 'things as they are', no matter how painful such recognition may be, before seeking consolation where consolation can authentically be found.[17] Accordingly, the letters report over and over again on symptoms and treatments, but they also turn to ballooning, a visit to Chatsworth, and various literary topics. For each correspondent, in short, Johnson devises variations on a theme.

Although it includes letters to thirteen friends, the sequence is dominated by extracts from letters to only two, Dr Richard Brocklesby and Sir Joshua Reynolds. The letters to Brocklesby, which begin the sequence, run from 20 July to 20 October, virtually the entire period of Johnson's absence from London. They open with an account of his journey to Lichfield and end by forecasting his death in the tones of the *Nunc dimittis*: 'Sir Joshua told me long ago, that my vocation was to publick life, and I hope still to keep my station, till GOD shall bid me *Go in peace*' (*Life* iv. 359). The letters to Reynolds, by retraversing the same period, fulfil the function of a flashback: we inhabit Johnson's sickroom more completely, and admire his fortitude more intensely, because we find ourselves back in July when we had reached October.

As originally designed, the Reynolds section of the sequence begins with a letter of 19 August that reports on the 'sensible

---

[17] 'Let us endeavour to see things as they are, and then enquire whether we ought to complain. Whether to see life as it is will give us much consolation I know not, but the consolation which is drawn from truth, if any there be, is solid and durable' (To Bennet Langton, 21 Sept. 1758, *Letters* i. 167).

remission' of Johnson's asthma. The next extract (2 September) continues to express optimism: 'My breath is easier, my nights are quieter, and my legs are less in bulk, and stronger in use' (*Life* iv. 367). The third and final letter, dated 18 September, completes the narrative of slow but steady improvement: 'I think, and I hope, am sure, that I still grow better.' This extract ends the original sampling of letters to Reynolds on a note of astringent humour. 'Do not write about the balloon, whatever else you may think proper to say': Johnson's mind, if not precisely soaring aloft, is not tethered to his body either (*Life* iv. 368).

By the time he completes his revisions, however, Boswell has doubled the length of the Reynolds section by adding extracts from three more letters. The first of these is dated 21 July, the last 2 October. One result of these additions is to intensify the flashback effect: we now re-experience virtually the entire ordeal, from Johnson's arrival in Lichfield through the time at Ashbourne to the last weeks in his native city. Another is to darken the tone of the whole. The first of the new extracts includes the gloomy observation, 'My sleep is little, my breath is very much encumbered, and my legs are very weak' (*Life* iv. 366). The final extract more than undercuts the optimism of the ballooning letters. By deciding both to begin and to end the revised section with stark reports of bodily decay, Boswell stresses the futility of Johnson's valetudinarian venture. Moreover, the revised conclusion to the Reynolds section echoes the resigned tone of the last words to Brocklesby: 'I do not at present grow better, nor much worse; my hopes, however, are somewhat abated, and a very great loss is the loss of hope, but I struggle on as I can' (*Life* iv. 368). By reshaping the penultimate section of this final epistolary sequence, Boswell prepares for the account of Johnson's last weeks, with its twofold emphasis on struggle and acquiescence.

Epistolary Pyrotechnics

Perhaps because it shows the Doctor 'upon stilts', Boswell chooses not to read Burney a passage from his epistolary *pièce de résistance*, the letter to Lord Chesterfield. However, this 'celebrated' document provides an ideal way of summarizing Boswell's arts of transmission and anticipating his manœuvres as tamer of Johnson. As publication of the *Life* approached, he went to unusual lengths to protect his literary property in the letter, causing a few copies to be printed in pamphlet form and entering them in the Stationers' Register. In addition, he included a special mention of it in the advertisement he sent to the *London Chronicle*.[18] As one might expect, he introduces the letter with extraordinary care, creating a narrative and interpretative frame that will enhance its brilliance as a stylistic tour de force, a biographical coup, and a landmark in the history of literary patronage.

Once again the manuscript bears witness to the fact that Boswell 'spared no pains . . . to fix' not a date in this instance but a letter—to create a frame that will set the letter off to best advantage. The most revealing of his adjustments occurs at the beginning of the paragraph that describes the failure of Chesterfield's propitiatory publicity: 'But [/all/ this was of no avail unless to shew the *invictum animum Catonis*>] this courtly artifice failed of its effect' (*Life MS* i. 187). In its earliest version, the sentence gathers its force from an allusion to Horace: the first ode of the second book, addressed to C. Asinius Pollio. As he revised, however, Boswell deleted the Horatian reference entirely. What might explain this deletion?

Boswell had turned to Horace before, at an equally important and delicate juncture, the passage that describes the infant

[18] *Literary Career*, 134–41; Baker, 418 n. 1.

Johnson's journey to London to be 'touched' for scrofula by Queen Anne:

> This touch however was without any effect. I ventured to say to him in allusion to the political principles in which he was educated and of which he ever retained some odour 'that his mother had not carried him far enough; She should have taken him to *Rome*.' (*Life MS* i. 22)

The tone of this passage is complex, combining as it does the serious and the playful in ways that are hard to pin down. Nonetheless, it is clear that Boswell is emphasizing his belief in Johnson's lifelong allegiance to the Stuart dynasty—an allegiance he shares, witness the reference to the healing powers that only the male Stuarts were thought to possess. In the margin of the manuscript at this juncture appears a deleted quotation from Horace's *Epistles*: 'Quo semel est imbuta recens servabit odorem—/ Testa diu': 'The jar will long keep the fragrance of what it was once steeped in when new' (1. 2. 69–70).[19] The fragrance of this quotation is preserved through the word 'odour'.

By contrast, no trace of Horace remains in the passage that introduces the Chesterfield letter. To intuit why this should be so we need to turn to the ode that Boswell remembered as he drafted the passage. At the beginning of his second book, Horace praises but also warns his friend Pollio, who has embarked on a risky enterprise, the writing of a history of the civil wars. Horace imagines the bloody scenes that Pollio's account will conjure up; these include the suicide of Cato:

> audire magnos iam videor duces,
> non indecoro pulvere sordidos,
>   et cuncta terrarum subacta
>   praeter atrocem animum Catonis. (ll. 21–4)[20]

---

[19] Horace, *Satires, Epistles and Ars Poetica*, trans. H. R. Fairclough (Cambridge, Mass.: Harvard Univ. Press, 1929), 267 (Loeb Classical Library).

[20] 'Already I seem to hear the shouts of mighty captains begrimed with no

It is probable, for reasons that we will be exploring in the next chapter, that the adjective *atrox* helped to activate in Boswell's mind the parallel between Johnson and Cato. This adjective can be translated in a variety of ways, ranging from 'violent', 'bloody', and 'savage' through 'alarming', 'fierce', and 'ruthless' to 'inflexible', 'stern', and 'stubborn'. In adapting the quotation, Boswell has half-censored it: *invictus* ('unconquered') stands in for *atrox*. Had it been allowed to remain, this Horatian tag with its altered adjective would have introduced a telling but decorous parallel between Johnson and Cato as men of high, severe, and unflinching principle. In the end, however, Boswell judges the risk too high: the remarks preceding this 'celebrated' letter must not be allowed to unbalance the contrast within the letter between the 'retired and uncourtly scholar' and the courtly but unreliable nobleman. Here too, Boswell has set his diamond in gold of Ophir.

Would Frances Burney have succumbed at Windsor if Boswell had read 'very well, and not caricature' from the Chesterfield letter? It seems unlikely, given her aversion to publicity of any kind. Would the inclusion of Johnson's 'beautiful billets' to her have made a difference to the biography? Undoubtedly, for they would have introduced the effervescent, playful, gallant Johnson we meet in the pages of Burney's *Diary*, thereby helping to compensate for the absence of letters to Hester Thrale. As Boswell himself said even before the *Life* appeared, the hero appears almost everywhere 'upon stilts'.

'Upon stilts' but not stilted, thanks in large measure to the letters that *are* included. The selection, the framing, and the linking of these letters accomplish all of Boswell's essential goals.

---

inglorious dust, and to see all the world subdued, except stern Cato's soul': Horace, *Odes and Epistles*, trans. C. E. Bennett (Cambridge, Mass.: Harvard Univ. Press, 1927), 109 (Loeb Classical Library).

They introduce multiple voices, topics, and perspectives. Unlike most of the conversations, they provide access to a Johnson who is not 'talking for victory'. They bridge reading time and remembered time: as Paul Alkon has so perceptively observed, to immerse oneself in the letters is to exist within the same 'temporal flow' as the original recipients.[21] They help to fulfil the promise of the title by 'exhibiting a view of literature and literary men in Great-Britain, for near half a century'. Finally, they equip Boswell to correct and surpass the works of his two principal rivals, Sir John Hawkins and Hester Thrale. At the beginning of the *Life*, Boswell criticizes Hawkins's biography for offering nothing more than a *'farrago'*, 'swelled out with long unnecessary extracts'. Toward the end of the biography, he argues that Thrale's *Anecdotes* purvey a distorted impression of Johnson by suggesting that he could 'hardly take the trouble to write a letter in favour of his friends' (*Life* i. 28, iv. 201). By practising his own, improved brand of 'the great epistolick art', Boswell contrives not a farrago but a phonograph, through which to transmit the Master's authentic voice.

[21] 'Within a factual work frequent intrusion of genuine, not invented, correspondence creates a series of shifts into real duration whose cumulative effect is further deceleration of temporal flow' (Alkon, 'Boswellian Time', 250).

5

Taming Johnson

Our enquiry into the design of the *Life of Johnson* enters its final phase as we attend to a portrait and a letter—the portrait by Reynolds that serves as a frontispiece and the 'celebrated letter' to Lord Chesterfield. In 'Representing Johnson' we took note of the fact that, as he neared the end of the biography, Boswell commissioned James Heath to engrave the portrait and then asked Reynolds to criticize Heath's efforts. According to Boswell, Reynolds 'suggested that the countenance was too young and not thoughtful enough. Mr. Heath therefore altered it . . . much to its advantage.'[1] Reynolds then finished the portrait so as to conform it to the engraving, and gave the portrait to Boswell, who in turn altered his original description in the manuscript of the *Life*. The passage in question glosses Johnson's first appearance to Boswell in Tom Davies's back parlour. The Ur-text is the entry from Boswell's *London Journal*, whose physical details are displaced by a gesture to the frontispiece: 'I found that I had a very [perfect/exact>] perfect idea of Johnson's [appearance/figure>] figure, from a picture of him by [/Sir Joshua/>] Sir Joshua Reynolds in the attitude of sitting in his easy=chair in deep meditation ∧soon after he had published his *Dictionary*∧' (*Life MS* i. 269).

What this description obscures, and what subsequent commentators have failed to notice, is that Reynolds depicts a scene of interrupted writing whose composition derives from scenes of interrupted reading. Johnson is seated at a desk, whose surface supports a volume of the *Dictionary*, an inkwell, and a sheaf of

---

[1] I quote from the annotated states of Heath's engraving in the Hyde Collection (Figs. 8, 9).

paper; in his right hand he grasps a quill pen, and with his left he holds the manuscript in place. His body is positioned at a slight angle to the picture plane, in order to suggest a posture of relaxation; his head is tilted and his eyes are unfocused. The severe geometry of book and desk acts as a visual counterpoint to the curve of the armchair, with its sloping back and its chequered fabric. The moment is one of deep reverie, and Reynolds emphasizes this fact by borrowing compositional elements from contemporary French painting—I think in particular of Greuze, who in the 1750s had begun to specialize in studies of sensibility via representations of the abstracted reader. In Reynolds's portrait, Johnson the abstracted writer dramatizes the tension between 'perusal' and 'curious reading'. I take these terms from Robert DeMaria Jr.'s *Samuel Johnson and the Life of Reading*, which argues that Johnson 'read in four distinct ways', and that 'perusal', or concentrated reading directed to such purposes as lexicography, alternated with 'curious reading', or non-critical absorption in works of the imagination.[2] Reynolds's study in suspended perusal might well be glossed by that haunting line from the 'Preface to the *Dictionary*': 'But these were the dreams of a poet doomed at last to wake a lexicographer.'[3] The tension between two kinds of mental states, two kinds of reading, and two kinds of writing is emphasized by the contrast between the two sides of Johnson's body (one rigid and compressed, the other expansive and relaxed), as well as the difference between the hands: the left is clenched, as if to restrain the work in progress, while the right is clasped loosely around the quill pen.[4]

[2] DeMaria Jr., *Samuel Johnson and the Life of Reading* (Baltimore: Johns Hopkins Univ. Press, 1997), 4–6.

[3] Preface to *A Dictionary of the English Language*, facsimile of 4th edn., 1773 (Beirut: Librairie du Liban, 1978), p. x.

[4] Compare Richard Wendorf's analysis in *The Elements of Life: Biography and Portrait-Painting in Stuart and Georgian England* (Oxford: Clarendon Press, 1990), 250–1.

Boswell chooses as his central icon a picture that licenses, advertises, and mirrors his own biographical tactics, as these tactics emerge from a close study of the *Life* manuscript. Remember that the engraver, guided by Boswell and Reynolds, has made the younger Johnson older and more thoughtful, creating thereby the aura of a sage 'in deep meditation'. Remember too that Boswell deletes the original passage from his journal, which emphasizes Johnson's 'dreadful appearance' and 'uncouth' voice, and substitutes a reference to the portrait. Both image and text, therefore, function as palimpsests or pentimenti—portraits through whose finished surfaces protrude bold, jagged originals.

And now to the Chesterfield letter. A supremely sophisticated document, it is also supremely aggressive—quite as aggressive as Johnson's defiant letter to James Macpherson. At the heart of the letter—its emotional as well as its structural centre—is a sentence more unsettling than we readily acknowledge. The rhetorical function of this sentence is to usher in the sardonic redefinition of 'patron', but it releases energies and creates disturbances in excess of this purpose: 'The Shepherd in Virgil grew at last acquainted with Love, and found him a Native of the Rocks.'[5] As John Wain observes, 'this [is] a superbly cadenced piece of writing, reminding us that we are dealing with a poet.'[6] We are, of course, dealing with two poets—Johnson and Virgil. The relationship between the two—that is to say, the allusive forcefield and its impact on the letter—is quite different from the preceding echoes of Boileau ('I . . . could not forbear to wish that I might boast myself Le Vainqueur du Vainqueur de la Terre') and Horace ('Seven years, My lord, have now past since I waited

[5] *Letters* i. 96.

[6] Wain, *Samuel Johnson* (New York: Viking Press, 1974), 176.

in your outward Rooms').[7] These two allusions mesh precisely
with Johnson's scheme of admonishment, while the reference
to Eclogue 8 threatens to tip the balance toward uncontrolled
feelings of betrayal and anger. Recall the context: Damon the
shepherd is singing of the despair of a jilted lover. In Paul Alpers's
translation:

> I know this thing called Love: on flinty rocks,
> Tmarus or Rhodope or wild Sahara
> Cradles a boy not of our blood or kind.
>
> .   .   .   .
>
> Taught by cruel Love, a mother stained her hands
> With her offspring's blood; mother, you too were cruel.
> Which was more savage, the mother or that boy?
> The boy was savage; mother, you too were cruel.[8]

The distinguishing epithet of Love is 'saevus', which translates
variously as 'harsh', 'savage', 'wild', 'fierce', 'untamed', 'ferocious'. By letting 'saevus Amor' into his letter, Johnson introduces tones of grief, lamentation, betrayal, and something like
ferocity. In so doing, he takes a great risk, for every other element
of the letter is devoted to proving that an 'uncourtly Scholar' can
beat the supreme courtier at his own game. We look through a
polished surface to see telegrams and anger.

To think about the portrait and the letter in tandem is to
reconsider the *Life* manuscript as a palimpsest. One discovery we
make is that Boswell documents continuities between a younger
and an older Johnson, but then ruptures or disguises these continuities. In its lower levels, the manuscript often gives us 'Savage
Johnson'—the Johnson of the early years in London, the Johnson who wandered with the author of 'The Wanderer'. What

---

[7] *Letters* i. 95.

[8] Alpers, *The Singer of the Eclogues* (Berkeley and Los Angeles: Univ. of California
Press, 1979), 49.

Boswell understands but chooses to downplay is that throughout his life Johnson remained 'saevus'—'saevus' in his religious and social life, 'saevus' in his politics, 'saevus' in his attitudes toward sexuality. One way of describing the achievement of the finished biography is to say that it holds in 'perilous balance' those forces that defined its protagonist from first to last.[9]

Boswell achieves this balance in several ways. Sometimes he will delete phrases and sentences that give away too much, as in this bleak summation of Johnson's troubled marital relations: 'The tenderness of his heart under a ferocious temperament will not be denied' (*Life MS* i. 174). Sometimes he will reformulate, as when a candid first thought, 'Of this dreary negation Johnson had all his life a miserable share,' is softened into something less bleak (*Life MS* i. 27). The most significant changes, however, occur not on an *ad hoc* basis but as part of a thorough recasting of entire episodes and even narrative sequences. I would like first to consider Boswell's handling of two episodes: the most important of the conversations about Hume and the account of Johnson's reaction to Bennet Langton's will. The revisions in these passages are significant but small-scale, unlike the changes to the episodes involving acts of physical and social aggression—three of which we will go on to analyse.

On 26 October 1769 Boswell performs an experiment on Johnson that enriches the biography but strains the friendship:

When we were alone, I introduced the subject of death, and endeavoured to maintain that the fear of it might be got over. I told him that David Hume said to me, he was not more uneasy to think he should *not be* after this life, than that he *had not been* before he began to exist. JOHNSON. 'Sir, if he really thinks so, his perceptions are disturbed; he is

---

[9] I take the phrase 'perilous balance' from the title of W. B. C. Watkins's pioneering study of Swift, Johnson, and Sterne (Princeton: Princeton Univ. Press, 1939).

mad: if he does not think so, he lies. He may tell you, he holds his finger in the flame of a candle, without feeling pain; would you believe him? When he dies, he at least gives up all he has.' BOSWELL. 'Foote, Sir, told me, that when he was very ill he was not afraid to die.' JOHNSON. 'It is not true, Sir. Hold a pistol to Foote's breast, or to Hume's breast, and threaten to kill them, and you'll see how they behave.' BOSWELL. 'But may we not fortify our minds for the approach of death?'—Here I am sensible I was in the wrong, to bring before his view what he ever looked upon with horrour; for although when in a celestial frame, in his 'Vanity of human Wishes,' he has supposed death to be 'kind Nature's signal for retreat,' from this state of being to 'a happier seat,' his thoughts upon this aweful change were in general full of dismal apprehensions. His mind resembled the vast amphitheatre, the Colisaeum at Rome. In the centre stood his judgement, which, like a mighty gladiator, combated those apprehensions that, like the wild beasts of the *Arena*, were all around in cells, ready to be let out upon him. After a conflict, he drove them back into their dens; but not killing them, they were still assailing him. To my question, whether we might not fortify our minds for the approach of death, he answered, in a passion, 'No, Sir, let it alone. It matters not how a man dies, but how he lives. The act of dying is not of importance, it lasts so short a time.' He added, (with an earnest look,) 'A man knows it must be so, and submits. It will do him no good to whine.' (*Life* ii. 106–7).

This conversation is one of the most thoroughly worked over in the entire manuscript. Boswell revises his draft to add details that quicken the drama of the intimate encounter and emphasize its revelatory significance. At the beginning, for example, he inserts the temporal and spatial marker 'When we were alone', and at the end the stage direction 'with an earnest look'. The most important changes, however, consist of two deletions and a substitution. In the first draft Johnson is recorded as saying, 'Sir, if he really thinks so his perceptions are disturbed; he is mad. If he does not think so he lies. Hume knows he lies. He may tell you he holds his finger in the flame of a candle, without feeling pain. Would you believe him?' In this first version, Johnson attributes to Hume a degree of bad faith, of obdurate perversity, that makes Hume's atheism all the more objectionable. Moreover, the repetition—'Hume knows he lies'—effectively eliminates the first possibility, that Hume is insane, and therefore strengthens our impression of Johnson's hostility: because the philosopher is not mad he is doubly bad and dangerous to know. The second cancellation identifies a possible reason for the ferocious antagonism: 'Garrick told me', Boswell records, 'that he believed him [Johnson] to be harrassed with doubts.' This sentence is thoroughly deleted, and the word 'doubts' so heavily scored through that it can only be deciphered with difficulty.

The two changes prepare for and correlate to the careful revision of Boswell's epic simile. The original version of this passage goes as follows:

His mind resembled the vast amphitheatre the Collosseum at Rome. In the center stands his Judgement like a mighty gladiator which combats doubts which like the wild beasts are all arround in cells/cages. He grumbles and growls while they foam and roar. They fight and he drives them into their dens, but never kills them, so that they are allways coming out again upon him. (*Life MS* ii. 56)

The change from 'doubts' in the first draft to 'apprehensions' in the final version has a subtle but decisive effect: it implies that Johnson's religious anxiety derives not from radical scepticism ('Is there an afterlife?') but from fear of judgment ('Will I be saved?'). The first Johnson is insecure in his Christianity, the second in his conviction of worthiness. In line with this shift of emphasis, Boswell reconsiders the nature of Johnson's gladiatorial combat. In the first version, the combat is ferocious, the struggle unceasing, the victory uncertain: 'He grumbles and growls while they foam and roar. They fight and he drives them into their dens, but never kills them, so that they are allways coming out again upon him.' In the original psychomachia, the allegorical force of 'Judgment' is subsumed into a personification so vivid that it runs away with the simile. Johnson is 'agonistes', granted, but the agon is so low down and dirty that our hero is reduced to the level of his savage antagonists. What is the difference, after all, between a gladiator who 'grumbles and growls' and a beast who 'foams and roars'? In the first draft, we might say, Johnson's 'nature is subdu'd to what it works in', whereas the revision presents him as a 'pattern of excelling nature'.

The episode of Bennet Langton's will-making functions as a comic pendant to the encounter we have just been considering. Boswell describes it as 'this most ludicrous exhibition'—and he exhibits Johnson in ways that only the manuscript can make completely clear. Here Boswell gives us a miniature problem comedy, which celebrates Johnson's laughter while interrogating its source and shrinking from its intensity. For there is something both tonic and morbid, endearing and bizarre, about this riotous midnight 'merriment':

I have known him at times exceedingly diverted at what seemed to others a very small sport. He now laughed immoderately, without any reason that we could perceive, at our friend's making his will; called him the *testator*, and added, 'I dare say, he thinks he has done a mighty thing. He won't stay till he gets home to his seat in the country, to produce this wonderful deed: he'll call up the landlord of the first inn on the road; and, after a suitable preface upon mortality and the uncertainty of life, will tell him that he should not delay making his will; and here, Sir, will he say, is my will, which I have just made, with the assistance of one of the ablest lawyers in the kingdom; and he will read it to him (laughing all the time). He believes he has made this will; but he did not make it: you, Chambers, made it for him. I trust you have had more conscience than to make him say, 'being of sound understanding;' ha, ha, ha! I hope he has left me a legacy. I'd have his will turned into verse, like a ballad.'

. . . Johnson could not stop his merriment, but continued it all the way till we got without the Temple-gate. He then burst into such a fit of laughter, that he appeared to be almost in a convulsion; and, in order to support himself, laid hold of one of the posts at the side of the foot pavement, and sent forth peals so loud, that in the silence of the night his voice seemed to resound from Temple-bar to Fleet-ditch. (*Life* ii. 261–2)

Reconstructing the evolution of the passage, we realize that Boswell intuitively grasps the importance of Johnson's unusual behaviour, but remains baffled by it. First he tries out an uneasy direction to the reader: 'Yet it must be very amusing and please us in a high degree to find that our mighty Moralist and Philologist could be so playful' (*Life MS* ii. 115). However, because he is not convinced that the episode is indeed 'amusing' and 'pleasant', he begs the question by substituting the adjective 'ludicrous', and restating his biographical manifesto: 'his pleasantry . . . is here preserved that my readers may be acquainted with the slightest occasional characteristicks of so eminent a man.'

Because there was no version of this episode recorded in his journal, Boswell worked directly from his notes, which preserve the following kernel:

He laughed immoderately at Langton. Langton the *testator*. I dare say he thinks he has done [a] thing a mighty thing. He won't stay till he gets home. He'll read his will to the Landlord of the first Inn on the road. Chambers you helped him. Did you put in being of sound understanding ha ha ha. I hope he has left me a Legacy. He should leave hatbands and gloves to all the Club. I'd have his will turned into verse like a Ballad. In this manner did he run on. Chambers accompanied us to the Temple Gate. Mr. Johnson could not stop his merriment. I cherished it crying 'Testator, Langton Longshanks.' *Johnson*: I wonder to whom he'll leave his legs? Ha ha ha making all Fleetstreet resound at the silent midnight hour.

Boswell makes the laughter resound in our ears as well. But

because it baffles and disturbs him, he adjusts the volume and the resonance. In the notes, and to a certain extent in the manuscript, the repeated 'ha ha ha' comes perilously close to 'howl howl howl'. Boswell's first choice of verb is 'bellowed forth', which prepares for the reference to 'such a fit of laughter, that he appeared to be almost in a convulsion'. The language here suggests an animal who is angry or in pain, or a victim of epilepsy; Boswell is remembering, I would argue, the 'foam and roar' of the Colosseum passage.

The final version drops the 'roar', and tames 'bellowed forth' into 'sent forth'. It also cuts 'He should leave hatbands and gloves to all the Club,' perhaps because the reference to the rituals of mourning blurs the focus on the self-aggrandizing rituals of will-making. But the most interesting deletion by far is the passage that reads: 'I cherished it [Johnson's laughter] calling out "Langton the testator, Langton Longshanks." This tickled his fancy so much that he roared out "I wonder to whom he'll leave his legs?"' (*Life MS* ii. 115–16). These deleted sentences make it clear that, once again, Boswell has chosen to perform an experiment upon Johnson, and that his 'cherishing' has a clinical dimension. The final result of an intervention that is designed to prolong and even to intensify Johnson's 'fit' is a bizarre image of dismemberment: 'I wonder to whom he'll leave his legs?' This, the wildest of Johnson's imaginings, threatens to make unusual behaviour seem pathological; it therefore disappears from the text.

Two additions to the first draft are likewise designed to emphasize Johnson's controlled self-awareness and even the comic sublimity of his 'exhibition'. Boswell expands 'He'll call up the Landlord of the first Inn on the road' into 'He'll call up the Landlord of the first Inn on the road, and after a suitable preface upon mortality and the uncertainty of life will tell him that he should not delay making his will.' The second clause causes Johnson to recognize that he as well as Langton is vulnerable to mockery: is not his stock in trade as moralist, after all, 'suitable prefaces upon mortality and the uncertainty of life'? The second addition situates his performance in the most urban of settings, the Strand, but a Strand that is dark and empty. The superimposition of 'w' upon 's' in the manuscript suggests that 'the silence of the night' began as the biblical 'watches of the night'.[10] Finally, the impression with which Boswell takes pains to leave us is not that of morbid pathology but of heroic energy: 'his voice seemed to resound from Temple-bar to Fleet-ditch.'

The two death-haunted episodes we have just been considering show Johnson responding with aggressive physicality to his fear of death. In the conversation about Hume, it is Boswell's simile that personifies Johnson's judgement, and by extension Johnson himself, as a tireless gladiator; the scene of laughter in the dark likewise dramatizes an eruption of energy that seems disproportionate to the cause, until we grasp the emotional subtext. At the beginning of the narrative for 1775, not long after this second episode, Boswell seizes the occasion of James Macpherson's menacing letter to provide additional examples of Johnson's combative spirit. The manuscript reveals that Boswell chose first to emphasize the threat posed by Macpherson, 'a robust highlander in the vigor of life',[11] as a way of introducing scenes of physical prowess. After inserting Johnson's epistolary riposte, Boswell adds: 'Mr Macpherson little knew the character of Dr. Johnson if he supposed that he could be easily intimidated; for no man was ever more remarkable for personal courage. He had indeed an aweful dread of death, or rather "of something after death" and what rational man who seriously thinks

---

[10] I owe this point to Dr Gordon Turnbull of the Yale Boswell Editions.

[11] This phrase does not survive into the final draft.

of quitting all that he has ever known can be without that dread. But his fear was [artificial>] from reflection his courage natural' (*Life MS* ii. 124). Then come six supporting examples. This portion of the text is so thoroughly revised, and therefore so difficult to make out, that Boswell had to request his daughter Veronica to prepare a fair copy for the printer. My reconstruction of the first draft goes as follows:

Mr. Beauclerk told me that one day at his house in the country when two large dogs were fighting/worrying, He went up to them and cuffed them asunder and at another time when cautioned not to put too many balls into a gun/charge a gun with too many balls lest it should burst, he put in six or seven, and fired it off against a wall. . . . Mr. Langton told me once at Oxford when they were swimming together, Mr. Langton shewed him a pool which was reckoned particularly dangerous; upon which he went/made for/plunged directly into it. And he himself confirmed to me a story which I was told how he was attacked in the street by four men, to whom he would not yield, but fought them fairly till the watch came up. . . . Mr. Garrick told me that one evening at the Play/in the Theatre at Lichfield a gentleman took possession of a chair which was placed for him between the side=scenes when he had quitted it for a moment. When he returned, he civilly demanded his seat, and the gentleman having refused it, he laid hold of him and tossed him chair and all/and the chair he sat on in to the pit. When Foote threatened to mimick him upon the stage he purchased a large oak cudgel declaring his resolution to beat him, which effectually checked the wantoness of the Wit. (*Life MS* ii. 124–5)

Though all these examples make it into print, all but one of the verbs of strenuous action disappear; those excised are 'cuffed', 'plunged', 'fought', and 'beat'. Consistent with his practice elsewhere, Boswell creates at first a hero whose capacity for violence is acted out in the most vigorous terms. But to control the interpretation of such powerful data, he must defuse the images he has conjured up, and yoke ambiguous behaviour to unambiguous virtues—in this case, to courage.

Johnson's displays of social ferocity are closely linked to his capacity for physical aggression. Boswell repeatedly takes note of the fact that Johnson considered himself (despite the adjective 'uncourtly' in the Chesterfield letter) to be a gentleman; moreover, his success in luring Johnson to the dinner with Wilkes depends upon his ability to exploit Johnson's commitment to refined social codes. However, this aspect of Boswell's portrait is often unconvincing because the sitter's behaviour is too complex and too emotionally charged to be thoroughly composed—'composed' in both the sense of 'pacified' and of 'arranged'.

Boswell has three ways of trying to convince the reader (and himself) that Johnson, despite occasional lapses, was essentially self-controlled and even courtly. The first and most direct is to insert personal testimonials that quite often contradict the evidence—as if a barrister were to attempt, in the act of summing up, to deny the import of testimony he himself had entered in the record. Boswell's second tactic is to document discrepancies between Johnson's idealized self-conception and his actual behaviour—but to do so gently, wryly, or even comically. The third is to suppress damning evidence completely. All three tactics can be observed at work in the narrative for 1776 and again for 1779. In the earlier narrative they fail egregiously, but in the later Boswell manages to 'compose' Johnson with almost complete success.

The notes and journal entries for Boswell's spring trip to London in 1776 show him drinking and wenching with truly feverish self-abandon. As Geoffrey Scott expresses it, his 'moral defences go down in a swirling black tide of passion'.[12] This

---

[12] *Private Papers of James Boswell from Malahide Castle in the Collection of Lt-Colonel Ralph Heyward Isham*, ed. Geoffrey Scott and Frederick A. Pottle, 18 vols. (privately printed, 1928–34), xi, p. iv. Henceforth cited as *BP*.

excursion ended in dalliance with Margaret Caroline Rudd and with painful reproaches from Johnson. When Boswell came to decant his personal archive into the biography, he found it impossible to tell certain stories at all, or even to preserve the evidence—witness the notable lacunae in the documentation (notes, journal, and *Life MS*).[13] The result is considerable damage to the biography, in terms both of completeness and artistic shaping. Though the notes would have allowed him to do so (the Wilkes playlet, after all, was created out of notes from this period), Boswell stops shaping his material dramatically; ironically, his excuse for this lapse runs counter to his most cherished biographical precept, that of minute 'particularity': 'To avoid a tedious minuteness, I shall group together what I have preserved of his conversation during this period also, without specifying each scene where it passed' (*Life* iii. 52). Further damage is done by Boswell's decision to sacrifice certain choice Johnsoniana in their entirety:

Take care of yourself. Don't drink. 'Tis as important for you as 'To be or not to be': To be in one's wits or not. You may when drunk do what you deserve to be hanged for next day. Every man is to take existence on the terms on which it is given to him. Yours is given to you on condition of your not using liberties which other people may. Don't talk of yourself or of me. . . . Don't make yourself and me a proverb. . . . I said, 'Thank you for all your kindness.' JOHNSON. 'You are very wellcome. Nobody repays it with more.'[14]

Because complete disclosure would have been too damaging, Boswell shrinks his account to a few brief sentences: 'On the evening of the next day I took leave of him, being to set out for Scotland. I thanked him with great warmth for all his kindness. "Sir (said he,) you are very welcome. Nobody repays it with

[13] The missing pages in the journal are those numbered 19–20, 25–34, 37–8; the missing pages in the *Life MS* are 608–12.

[14] *BP* xi. 289. See Frank Brady's discussion in *Later Years*, 135.

more"' (*Life* iii. 80). In the published *Life,* Boswell then launches directly into a vehement and extended tribute to Johnson as social being. This tribute begins and ends by insisting upon Johnson's civility, on his gentlemanly behaviour:

How very false is the notion which has gone round the world of the rough, and passionate, and harsh manners of this great and good man. . . . On the contrary, the truth is, that by much the greatest part of his time he was civil, obliging, nay, polite in the true sense of the word; so much so, that many gentlemen, who were long acquainted with him, never received, or even heard a strong expression from him. (*Life* iii. 80–1)

Yet the record of Johnsonian encounters during the previous two months abounds with precisely such 'strong expressions'—a jarring contrast that helps to undermine the rhetorical effect of the tributes and even to cast doubt on the candour of the biographer. Neither suppression, abbreviation, nor compensation suffices to align what is told with how it is interpreted.

A similar move, whereby Boswellian accolade substitutes for Johnsonian reproof, occurs in the narrative for 28 March 1776. This time Boswell both suppresses and redistributes his raw materials. In the original entry, he begins by recording the most vehement of all Thomas Sheridan's outbursts: 'We journeyed on very well. I talked of Sheridan's saying and persisting to say that Dr. Johnson had a black heart becase Dr. Johnson had said, "If they have given him a pension, it is time for me to give up mine."' This passage disappears, as does the direct report of 'black' behaviour that ends the original journal entry: 'The rattling of the Chaise today prevented me from hearing Dr. Johnson talk. I told him so. "Then," said he, "you may go hang yourself." It is strange when such a sally bursts from him.'[15] In

---

[15] *Boswell: The Ominous Years 1774–1776,* ed. Charles Ryskamp and Frederick A. Pottle (New York: McGraw-Hill, 1963), 302.

place of these two passages, Boswell inserts a paean of praise—
a substitution so striking that it cannot help but register as an
act of repression and atonement. The paean begins by denying
the very behaviour that the journal has recorded: 'It was an
undoubted proof of his good sense and good disposition that he
was never querulous, never inveighing against the times, as is so
common, when superficial minds are on the fret.'[16] 'Undoubted'
helps to signal Boswell's doubts and the strain that comes from
effortful compensation.

As such collation of journal and manuscript makes clear,
Boswell is protesting too much because he is arguing with himself. But even without access to his workshop, the reader of the
published *Life* registers a shrillness in tone and a lapse in timing.
Even more discordant notes are struck when evidence is not
suppressed or softened but interpreted—and the interpretation
runs counter to the evidence. Such is the case with an anecdote
involving Gibbon.

No man was a more attentive ∧and nice∧ observer of behaviour in
those in whose company he happened to be, than Johnson, or however strange it may seem to many, had a higher [value>] estimation
of its refinements. Lord Eliot informs me that one day when Johnson
and he were at dinner at a gentleman's house in London ∧when Lord
Chesterfield's letters were mentioned∧ Johnson surprised the company
by this sentence. 'Every man of any education would rather be called
a rascal than be accused of deficiency in the graces.' Mr. Gibbon who
was present turned to a Lady who knew Johnson well and lived much
with him and in his sly manner, tapping his box addressed her thus,
'Don't you think Madam ∧(looking toward Johnson)∧ that among all
your acquaintance you could find one exception?' The Lady smiled,
and seemed to acquiesce.[17]

Two alterations in this passage further complicate Boswell's

[16] MS 552ᵛ: Houghton Library, Harvard University.
[17] MS 586ᵛ: Houghton Library, Harvard University.

recuperative tactics. First, the addition in manuscript of the word 'nice' stretches the opening claim to breaking point; second, the change in proof from 'sly' to 'quaint' subverts the ostensible point of the story by making Gibbon's incredulous response more rather than less appealing.

The narrative for spring 1776 is one of the few cases in the *Life* where we can convict Boswell of radical misjudgement. On most occasions, he knew how to calibrate means to ends by omitting certain data and refining others. The account of Johnson's quarrel with Beauclerk in 1779 had the potential to backfire disastrously by displacing the reader's sympathy from aggressor (Johnson) to victim (Beauclerk). Though Boswell's notes offered him the materials for another playlet, complete with prologue and epilogue, he chose to work up only the central episode. The potential prologue consisted of a conversation with Beauclerk about Johnson's bearishness:

> We talked of Dr. Johnson's way of saying rough and severe things to people in company. Beauclerk said he wondered it had never happened that some violent man [had not struck him.] He wished to see it to teach Johnson how to behave. 'To be sure, a man would be a brute who did it. But it would do good.' 'O no,' said I, 'at his age.' Beauclerk answered, 'At his age he should be thinking of better things than to abuse people.'[18]

Boswell's concluding observation, 'this was the most agreeable interview I ever had with Beauclerk', completely undermines his demurral ('O no, at his age'). A potential epilogue, in which Boswell converses with Burke after the confrontation, makes Johnson's hostility even more obvious:

> I told Burke of contest between Johnson and Beauclerk. Said he, 'Between Fury and Malevolence.' I. 'The <bear and> —what is a

---

[18] Notes for 15 Apr. 1779; see *Boswell, Laird of Auchinleck 1778–1782*, ed. Joseph W. Reed and Frederick A. Pottle (New York: McGraw-Hill, 1977), 83.

small animal <that stands ground?"> BURKE. 'A polecat.' BOSWELL. 'Is <that spirit>ed enough?' 'O yes,' said Burke. BOSWELL. 'Palmer wondered how I could help Johnson's <fury a>long.' BURKE. 'He'd rather see <your e> xecut[ion] than none.' 'But,' <said I, 'he> recovers me.' 'Yes,' said <Burke, 'he ta>kes you to [the] Humane Society [afterwards.] He has it in his breast.'[19]

By contrast, Boswell repeatedly goes out of his way (in the Paper Apart that records the actual confrontation) to diffuse the effect of Johnson's 'fury'. He cuts a parenthetical statement that supports Beauclerk. He moderates his interpretation of Johnson's behaviour, ascribing it first to anger but then to resentment and a disinclination to be considered a coward. Finally and most importantly, he stresses the fact that Johnson stayed with Beauclerk 'a long time' after their dispute, as a means of making amends and putting their friendship back on a relaxed footing. Through such omissions and revisions, Boswell retains aesthetic control over the episode, distilling his raw ambivalence into nuanced ambiguity.

Thus far we have been examining Boswell's arts of management as applied to Johnson's religious life, his ethical commitments, and his social code. No investigation into the biographer's designs upon his savage protagonist would be complete without a look at the treatment of politics and sexuality.

As we noticed in the second chapter, Boswell imagines for Johnson a career as a Member of Parliament, and surmises that in the House of Commons he would have exerted a 'ready force of mind', as well as 'strength . . . of expression' and 'sarcastical keeness' (*Life MS* ii. 65). These qualities Boswell also locates in Johnson's responses to three highly charged political issues: the rebellion in America, Wilkite 'patriotism', and the Jacobite cause. He pays special attention to the four tracts of the 1770s,

---

[19] Notes for 18 April 1779; see ibid. 92.

finding in them what he calls 'an extreme coarseness of contemptuous abuse' (*Life MS* ii. 59). Nonetheless, he consistently tones down the most vehement of Johnson's opinions, as well as monitoring his own commentary on those opinions. Accordingly, he cancels in proof a fascinating passage that sheds light on the conclusion of *The False Alarm*: 'Indeed I [am well/was>] am well informed that there was struck out from it an expression still more degrading than any that [now remain/remain/are left>] now remain "Had government been [overturned/changed>] overturned by this faction England had died of a *Thyrasis*" ' (*Life MS* ii. 59).[20] Boswell also declines to use a comparable anecdote that appears in his notebook:

Johnson had a sovereign contempt for Wilkes and his party, whom he looked upon as a mere rabble. 'Sir,' said he, 'had Wilkes's mob prevailed against Government, this nation had died of *phthiriasis* . . . The expression, *Morbus pediculosus*, as being better known, would strike more. *Lousy disease* may be put in a parenthesis.'[21]

Even in parenthetical form, however, 'lousy disease' is eradicated, as is Boswell's candid opinion of Johnson's response to the Americans: 'He seemed to me instead of a dexterous Champion to be a furious Bull turned loose to trample down and toss and gore the Colonists and all their friends' (*Life MS* ii. 131). When he rampages in this fashion, Johnson reminds Boswell not only of a 'furious Bull' but also of an erupting volcano: 'he said "I am willing to love all mankind *except an American*"; and his inflammable corruption [bursting into/taking>] bursting into horrid fire he "breathed out slaughter" calling them "Rascals Robbers Pirates," and crying ∧out∧ he'd "burn and destroy" ' (MS 692). But just as Boswell decides not to risk turning

---

[20] *phthiriasis*: 'a morbid condition of the body in which lice multiply excessively, causing extreme irritation' (*OED*).

[21] Waingrow, 257 n. 10.

Johnson into a wild beast, so he restrains his commentary on Johnson the firebreather: 'During this tempest, I sat in great uneasiness, lamenting his [ferocity/violence>] heat of temper till by degrees . . . I diverted his attention to other topicks' (MS 692).

For the past decade, Boswell has been enlisted on both sides in an increasingly ill-tempered debate over Johnson's putative Jacobitism. The two chief proponents of the Jacobite interpretation, Howard Erskine-Hill and J. C. D. Clark, have both argued that the manuscript of the *Life* is an important source for understanding Johnson's undisguised opinions, and that the edition of the manuscript will clarify several vexed questions. Clark, for example, declares that 'a full discussion of the evidential problem must await the publication of the complex manuscript draft'.[22] And Erskine-Hill observes, 'Boswell can massage his evidence . . . and until the intermediate manuscript of *The Life of Johnson* has been published we cannot be sure how far Boswell manipulated his materials.' This statement suggests little patience for, or understanding of, Boswell's biographical craftsmanship, though Erskine-Hill does go on to observe: 'In any case, Boswell was certainly not trying to be a strictly objective academic biographer, and should not be treated as such.'[23] Here Erskine-Hill and Donald Greene, chief denouncer of 'Boswellizing', find themselves unexpectedly in agreement.[24]

One person's 'massaging' and 'manipulation' is another's 'artistic control'. *Pace* Erskine-Hill and Greene, I would argue that the manuscript does not provide evidence that would suffice

[22] Clark, *Samuel Johnson: Literature, Religion and English Cultural Politics from the Restoration to Romanticism* (Cambridge: Cambridge Univ. Press, 1994), 9 n. 31.

[23] Erskine-Hill, 'Johnson the Jacobite? A Response to the New Introduction to Donald Greene's *The Politics of Samuel Johnson*', *Age of Johnson*, 7 (1996), 5.

[24] Greene, *The Politics of Samuel Johnson*, 2nd edn. (Athens: Univ. of Georgia Press, 1990), p. lxii.

to clarify the debate. The reason it does not offer such testimony is that, assessed as historical data, all the references to Jacobitism are ambiguous at best.[25] Analysed from the literary vantage point, by contrast, they unambiguously show Boswell shaping his materials in accordance with one fundamental goal: to mute the bellowing of the 'furious Bull'. In short, both camps have been guilty of converting ambiguities into certainties, and of blurring the distinction between fundamentally different kinds of evidence. The result is confusion and continuing acrimony.

Both the slipperiness of the data and the consistency of Boswell's biographical procedures will become apparent if we consider three representative alterations in the manuscript. The first of these is a brief mention of *Marmor Norfolciense*: 'To this supposed Prophecy he gave a [full *del*] Commentary making each expression apply to the times, with warm [jacobite>] anti-hannoverian zeal' (*Life MS* i. 98). The second occurs in a discussion of Johnson's anonymous dedications: '*Johnson*. "Why I have dedicated to the Royal Family all round, that is to say to the last Royal Family" ' (*Life MS* ii. 93). This sentence was altered (presumably in first proof) to read, ' "Why I have dedicated to the Royal Family all round, that is to say, to the last generation of the Royal Family." ' The third adapts a passage from the journal: 'He imputed the present anarchy in Government in a good measure to the Revolution. "For," said he, "this Hanoverian family is *isolée* here." '[26] The passage in the manuscript reads, 'He talked with regret and indignation of the factious opposition to Government [in Britain>] at this time and imputed it in a [good>] great measure to the Revolution. "Sir" (said he in a

---

[25] The most ambiguous fact of all is the lacuna that robs us of the discussion of Johnson's pension. See *Life MS* i. 261 n. 6.

[26] *Boswell: The Applause of the Jury 1782–1785*, ed. Irma S. Lustig and Frederick A. Pottle (New York: McGraw-Hill, 1981), 74 (21 Mar. 1783).

low voice having come nearer to me ∧while his old prejudices seemed to be fermenting in his mind∧) this Hannoverian family is *isolée* here' (MS 863).

In all three cases, the attempt to establish the *political* rationale for the changes is doomed to frustration. In the first instance, the alteration from 'jacobite' to 'antihannoverian' might be considered a cover-up or a subtle ideological reinterpretation. Likewise, the change from 'the last Royal Family' to 'the last generation of the Royal Family' could be viewed as censorship—Boswell's suppression of a subversive ambiguity. The third example has been interpreted by Howard Erskine-Hill as a privileged revelation: 'These remarks are dramatically effective because they are a *confidence*; the "low voice" and the drawing nearer help us to see an old man uttering his innermost convictions to an intimate friend.'[27] Erskine-Hill's analysis conflates astute critical commentary with an unwarranted assumption about the political content of the statement: Boswell's revisions do indeed help us to 'see an old man'—I would emphasize the 'old'—but they do not allow us to assign Johnson's comment the status of 'innermost conviction'. Only by restricting our analysis to the tonal or dramatic impact of Boswell's changes can we derive clear and helpful conclusions about his biographical designs.

Like the evidence we have been considering thus far, passages in the manuscript that bear on Johnson's sexuality consist of local deletions and revisions, as well as the careful reworking of entire structural blocks. Boswell introduces, reconsiders, and occasionally suppresses three interlocking topics: Johnson's sexual drive,

[27] Erskine-Hill, 'The Political Character of Samuel Johnson', in Isobel Grundy (ed.), *Samuel Johnson: New Critical Essays* (London: Vision, 1984), 116. For Greene's assessment of Erskine-Hill's analysis, see *The Politics of Samuel Johnson*, 2nd edn., pp. xlvi–xlvii.

his interest in female sexual behaviour, and his preoccupation with the links between sexuality and property.

As we now know well, 'There never was a man who had stronger amorous inclinations than Dr. Johnson.' I quote from the manuscript Boswell called 'Extraordinary Johnsoniana—*Tacenda*', the record of his interview with Elizabeth Desmoulins, to whom Johnson was powerfully attracted but whom he refrained from seducing.[28] In composing the *Life*, Boswell chose to ignore Mrs Desmoulins's testimony, just as he chose to ignore the evidence of Johnson's diaries and prayers, and to dismiss 'the dark hints' of Sir John Hawkins.[29] When Johnson is allowed to express sexual desire, the context is always somewhat comic, as in Garrick's story of the amorous young bridegroom and the anecdote of Johnson during the production of *Irene*. The version we know, 'I'll come no more behind your scenes, David, for the silk-stockings and white bosoms of your actresses excite my amorous propensities', begins in the manuscript as 'I'll come no more behind your scenes David; for the silk=stockings and white bubbies of your actresses excite my genitals' (*Life MS* i. 146–7, 427). The difference between 'amorous propensities' and 'genitals' indexes the difference between the two Johnsons, tamed and untamed. What Boswell chooses to tell is the story of a young Johnson whose 'propensities', though ardent, were almost always licit (the only improprieties at which he is prepared to hint are those that result from Johnson's association with the 'licentious' Savage). As he grows older, this virtuous young man plays the role of a flirtatious but essentially harmless *cavaliere servente*—all real passion convincingly spent.

[28] *Applause of the Jury*, ed. Lustig and Pottle, 110–13.

[29] See the essays by Donald and Mary Hyde ('Dr. Johnson's Second Wife') and by Frederick A. Pottle ('The Dark Hints of Sir John Hawkins and Boswell') in Frederick W. Hilles (ed.), *New Light on Dr. Johnson* (New Haven: Yale Univ. Press, 1959), 133–62.

Boswell is likewise careful to mute Johnson's commentary on the sexual drive and sexual conduct of women. Boswell understood that Johnson's insistence on the regulation—social, moral, and legal—of female sexuality derived from his conviction of its strength. For Johnson, women were weak of body and mind but strong of appetite. In a conversation recorded only in Boswell's notes, he discusses the Queen of Hungary:

The difference between Men and Women was mentioned. Some one said the Queen of Hungary was as able as any man. JOHNSON. 'Sir, she would have cut off her thumbs to be a man. I'm afraid where there is no education, as in savage countries, men will have the upper hand. True, bodily strength contributes. But the government is by mind. When it comes to dry understanding, Men get the better.'[30]

Inferior as they are in 'dry understanding', women use their bodies to subjugate men. When John Taylor's wife left him, Johnson wrote to his old friend:

You enquire what the fugitive Lady has in her power. She has, I think, nothing in her power but to return home and mend her behaviour. . . . Nature has given women so much power that the Law has very wisely given them little.[31]

Two revealing conversations, both of them extensively revised, articulate the link in Johnson's thinking between the power of 'Nature' and the power of 'Law'. Both are conversations about adultery, and both can be read as predictable endorsements of a double standard: infidelity in a man is wrong but forgivable—and even, under certain circumstances, almost endearing—while infidelity in a woman is wrong and unforgivable under any circumstances.

---

[30] Notes for 8 May 1776, as expanded by Geoffrey Scott and Frederick Pottle in *BP* xi. 272.

[31] *Letters* i. 228 (to John Taylor, 18 Aug. 1763).

In the earlier conversation, Boswell rewrites a sentence that provides startling insight into Johnson's view of female chastity. The version that makes its way into print is vehement but decorous: 'I asked him if it was not hard that one deviation from Chastity should so absolutely ruin a young woman. *Johnson.* "Why no Sir. It is the great principle which she is taught. When she has given up that principle, she has given up every notion of female honour and virtue, which are all included in chastity" ' (*Life MS* ii. 30). In the original version, Johnson minces no words: 'I asked him if it was not hard that one deviation from chastity should so absolutely ruin a woman. JOHNSON. "Why, no, Sir; the great principle which every woman is taught is to keep her legs together." '[32] The brutality of both style and substance reflects a belief in women's natural propensity to do the opposite—a propensity that requires the strongest sanctions. It is a striking fact that Boswell not only deletes the sentence but adds an entirely new paragraph, which nervously (and rather sanctimoniously) glosses the incident:

Here he discovered that acute discrimination, that solid judgment, and that knowledge of human nature, for which he was upon all occasions remarkable. Taking care to keep in view the moral and religious duty, as understood in our nation, he shewed clearly from reason and good sense, the greater degree of culpability in the one sex deviating from it than the other; and, at the same time, inculcated a very useful lesson as to *the way to keep him*. (*Life* ii. 56)[33]

Boswell's final reference to Arthur Murphy's play *The Way to Keep Him* completes the distancing manœuvre by straining for a comic conclusion.

This decidedly uncomic discussion of adultery opens with

[32] *Boswell in Search of a Wife 1766–1769*, ed. Frank Brady and Frederick A. Pottle (London: Heinemann, 1957), 167 (28 Mar. 1768).

[33] This paragraph appears for the first time in the 2nd edition.

Johnson's declaration, 'Confusion of progeny constitutes the Essence of the crime; and therefore a woman who breaks her marriage vows is so much more criminal than a man who does it. A man to be sure is criminal in the sight of GOD. But he does not do his wife a very material injury' (*Life MS* ii. 29). Johnson's claim opens up two perspectives on adultery, the religious or moral on the one hand and the material or financial on the other. For 'confusion of progeny' leads inevitably to 'confusion of inheritance' and 'confusion of property'.

In this exchange the link between the two kinds of confusions remains implicit, but later in the *Life* it is clearly revealed. One of the cancels we discussed in the first chapter yields the following provocative but decorous passage:

I mentioned to him a dispute between a friend of mine and his lady, concerning conjugal infidelity, which my friend maintained was by no means so bad in the husband as in the wife. JOHNSON. 'Your friend was in the right, Sir. Between a man and his maker it is a different question; but between a man and his wife, a husband's infidelity is nothing. They are connected by children, by fortune, by serious considerations of community. Wise married women don't trouble themselves about infidelity in their husbands.' BOSWELL. 'To be sure there is a great difference between the offence of infidelity in a man and that of his wife.' JOHNSON. 'The difference is boundless. The man imposes no bastards upon his wife.' (*Life* iii. 406)

The last sentence, which Boswell initially marked for deletion and then restored, gives some clue as to the frankness of the original exchange.[34] The first of the excised passages reveals intimate facts about Johnson's marriage:

'Wise married women. . . . detest a mistress but don't mind a whore. My Wife told me I might lye with as many women as I pleased provided

---

[34] The cancelled leaf, with Boswell's directions to the compositor, is in the Hyde Collection.

I *loved* her alone.' BOSWELL. 'She was not in earnest.' JOHNSON. 'But she was. Consider Sir how gross it is in a wife to complain of her husband's going to other women ∧merely as women∧. It is that she has not enough of [tail>] what she would be ashamed to avow.' BOSWELL. 'And was Mrs. Johnson then so liberal ∧Sir∧?' (MS 793)

Boswell's question ('And was Mrs. Johnson then so liberal?') daringly recognizes the autobiographical dimension to Johnson's dicta; moreover, Johnson's ostentatious refusal to answer the question effectively confirms that dimension. The second deletion, though much shorter, is perhaps even more significant. Originally 'the difference is boundless' was separated from 'the man imposes no bastards upon his wife' by an interjection from Boswell, 'Yes, boundless as property and honours.' The need for sexual fidelity in women is thereby connected to the propagation of legitimate sons, whose legitimacy helps to preserve the social and economic order. A third deletion makes even clearer Johnson's belief in the dangerous consequences of female 'looseness':

Boswell. 'Suppose ∧Sir∧ a woman to be of [such a constitution that she does not like it/conjugal intercourse, she has no right to complain that/if her husband goes elsewhere>] a ∧very cold∧ constitution, has she any right to complain of her husband's infidelity?' *Johnson.* ∧Sir∧ If she refuses [it *del*] she has not right to complain.' *Boswell.* [Then as oft as a man's wife refuses, he may mark it down>] 'Then Sir according to your doctrine, [upon every such/on every such>] upon every such occasion a man may make a note in his pocket=book, and do as he pleases with a [safe/good>] safe conscience.' *Johnson.* 'Nay Sir ∧this is wild indeed.∧ You must consider [to whore is wrong>] fornication is a crime in a single man; and [one>] you cannot have more liberty by being married.' (MS 793–4)

The final sentence, had it survived into the published text, might well have contained a parenthetical 'smiling' or 'slyly', for Johnson is turning the tables on Boswell as surely as he does in the presence of Wilkes. Though he recognizes the power of the scene, Boswell cannot bring himself to release it to the public in unexpurgated form. Nonetheless, he keenly regrets such an ostentatious act of taming, witness the letter to Malone that comments on the cancel: 'I wonder how you and I admitted this to the public eye. . . . It is however mighty good stuff.'[35]

As we noticed in 'Representing Johnson', the sacrificing of 'mighty good stuff' for the sake of 'the public eye' continued right through the shaping of the final 'Character', where the public eyes Johnson for one last time (Figs. 1, 2). In this climactic phase of composition, Boswell adheres to his practice throughout, first releasing and then restraining a harshly xenophobic Johnson:

[He suffered his mind to be possessed by prejudices unworthy of a great mind, having an unreasonable contemptuous aversion to his fellow subjects who were not english, and for all foreigners in general>] . . . Nor can it be denied that he indulged prejudices unworthy of a great mind against his fellow subjects in Ireland and Scotland, [and] for foreigners in general. (MS 1040)

To avoid panegyric yet inspire reverence, Boswell settles finally on a more general admission, which he connects to a tribute: 'Nor can it be denied, that he had many prejudices; which, however, frequently suggested many of his pointed sayings, that rather shew a playfulness of fancy than any settled malignity' (*Life* iv. 426). In this final revision, prejudice is construed as the source of playfulness, ferocity as the engine of fancy.

We conclude where we began, with the letter to Lord Chesterfield and the Reynolds frontispiece. As this selective excavation of its layers has suggested, the *Life* manuscript reveals how consistently Boswell exhibits, but then restrains, a Johnson who is 'a Native of the Rocks'. Such restraint is necessary if Boswell is to fulfil his biographical project—to interpret Johnson's weaknesses under the aspect of his strengths, to create a

---

[35] Baker, 400–1; see Ch. 1 above.

hero who is compellingly 'agonistes'. The figure that emerges from the layered text is the subject of the portrait that ushers in the text. My argument is encapsulated by the contrast between the two hands, one clenched and the other relaxed, and by the engraver's transformation of savage into sage.

BIBLIOGRAPHY

ALKON, PAUL K., 'Boswellian Time', *Studies in Burke and his Time*, 14 (Spring 1973), 239–56.

BOSWELL, JAMES, *Boswell in Search of a Wife 1766–1769*, ed. Frank Brady and Frederick A. Pottle (London: Heinemann, 1957).

——*Boswell: The Ominous Years 1774–1776*, ed. Charles Ryskamp and Frederick A. Pottle (New York: McGraw-Hill, 1963).

——*Boswell in Extremes 1776–1778*, ed. Charles McC. Weis and Frederick A. Pottle (New York: McGraw-Hill, 1970).

——*Boswell, Laird of Auchinleck 1778–1782*, ed. Joseph W. Reed and Frederick A. Pottle (New York: McGraw-Hill, 1977).

——*Boswell: The Applause of the Jury 1782–1785*, ed. Irma S. Lustig and Frederick A. Pottle (New York: McGraw-Hill, 1981).

——*Boswell: The English Experiment 1785–1789*, ed. Irma S. Lustig and Frederick A. Pottle (New York: McGraw-Hill, 1986).

——*Boswell: The Great Biographer 1789–1795*, ed. Marlies K. Danziger and Frank Brady (New York: McGraw-Hill, 1989).

——*Boswell's Life of Johnson*, ed. G. B. Hill, rev. L. F. Powell, 6 vols. (Oxford: Clarendon Press, 1934–50; vols. v–vi, rev. 1964).

——*Boswell's Journal of* A Tour to the Hebrides, ed. Frederick A. Pottle and Charles Bennett (New York: Viking, 1936).

——*James Boswell's* Life of Johnson: *An Edition of the Original Manuscript in Four Volumes* (Edinburgh: Edinburgh Univ. Press and Yale Univ. Press, 1994–). Vol. i: *1709–1765*, ed. Marshall Waingrow; vol. ii: *1766–1776*, ed. Bruce Redford, with Elizabeth Goldring.

——*Private Papers of James Boswell from Malahide Castle in the Collection of Lt-Colonel Ralph Heyward Isham*, ed. Geoffrey Scott and Frederick A. Pottle, 18 vols. (privately printed, 1928–34).

BOSWELL, JAMES, *The Correspondence and Other Papers of James Boswell Relating to the Making of the* Life of Johnson, ed. Marshall Waingrow, 2nd edn. (Edinburgh: Edinburgh Univ. Press. and Oxford Univ. Press, 2001).

—— *The Correspondence of James Boswell with David Garrick, Edmund Burke, and Edmond Malone*, ed. Peter S. Baker et al. (London: Heinemann, 1986).

BRADY, FRANK, *James Boswell: The Later Years 1769–1795* (New York: McGraw-Hill, 1984).

DEMARIA JR., ROBERT, *Samuel Johnson and the Life of Reading* (Baltimore: Johns Hopkins Univ. Press, 1997).

DOWLING, WILLIAM C., *Language and Logos in Boswell's* Life of Johnson (Princeton: Princeton Univ. Press, 1981).

EDEL, LEON, *Writing Lives: Principia Biographica* (New York: W. W. Norton, 1984).

FRANK, JOSEPH, *The Idea of Spatial Form* (New Brunswick, NJ: Rutgers Univ. Press, 1991).

GASKELL, PHILIP, *A New Introduction to Bibliography* (New York: Oxford Univ. Press, 1972).

GREENE, DONALD J., 'Reflections on a Literary Anniversary', *Queen's Quarterly*, 70 (1963), 193–208. Reprinted in abridged form in James L. Clifford (ed.), *Twentieth-Century Interpretations of Boswell's Life of Johnson* (Englewood Cliffs, NJ: Prentice-Hall, 1970), 97–103.

—— ''Tis a Pretty Book, Mr. Boswell, But—', *Georgia Review*, 32 (1978), 17–43. Reprinted in expanded form in John A. Vance (ed.), *Boswell's* Life of Johnson*: New Questions, New Answers* (Athens: Univ. of Georgia Press, 1985), 110–46.

—— *The Politics of Samuel Johnson*, 2nd edn. (Athens: Univ. of Georgia Press, 1990).

HEILAND, DONNA, 'Remembering the Hero in Boswell's *Life of Johnson*', in Greg Clingham (ed.), *New Light on Boswell* (Cambridge: Cambridge Univ. Press, 1991).

HILLES, FREDERICK W. (ed.), *New Light on Dr. Johnson* (New Haven: Yale Univ. Press, 1959).

—— *Portraits by Sir Joshua Reynolds* (New York: McGraw-Hill, 1952).

HOLMES, RICHARD, 'Biography: Inventing the Truth,' in John

Batchelor (ed.), *The Art of Literary Biography* (Oxford: Clarendon Press, 1995), 15–25.

JOHNS, ADRIAN, *The Nature of the Book: Print and Knowledge in the Making* (Chicago: Univ. of Chicago Press, 1998).

JOHNSON, SAMUEL, *The Rambler*, ed. W. J. Bate and Albrecht B. Strauss, 3 vols. (New Haven: Yale Univ. Press, 1969).

—— *The Letters of Samuel Johnson*, ed. Bruce Redford, 5 vols. (Princeton: Princeton Univ. Press, The Hyde Edition, 1992–4).

—— *The Letters of Samuel Johnson*, ed. R. W. Chapman, 3 vols. (Oxford: Clarendon Press, 1952).

Johnson and Boswell Revised (Oxford: Clarendon Press, 1928).

KERNAN, ALVIN, *Printing Technology, Letters & Samuel Johnson* (Princeton: Princeton Univ. Press, 1987).

LUSTIG, IRMA S., 'Fact into Art: James Boswell's Notes, Journals, and the *Life of Johnson*', in John D. Browning (ed.), *Biography in the 18th Century* (New York: Garland, 1980), 128–46.

—— 'Facts and Deductions: The Curious History of Reynolds's First Portrait of Johnson, 1756', *Age of Johnson*, 1 (1987), 161–80.

McGANN, JEROME J., *A Critique of Modern Textual Criticism* (Charlottesville: Univ. of Virginia Press, 1992).

McKENZIE, D. F., 'Printers of the Mind: Some Notes on Bibliographical Theories and Printing-House Practices', *Studies in Bibliography*, 22 (1969), 1–75.

—— *Bibliography and the Sociology of Texts: The Panizzi Lectures, 1985* (London: The British Library, 1986). Reprinted by Cambridge University Press, 1999.

MAXTED, IAN, *The London Book Trades 1775–1800* (London: Dawson, 1977).

MOLIN, SVEN ERIC, 'Boswell's Account of the Johnson–Wilkes Meeting', *SEL* 3 (1963), 307–22.

MOXON, JOSEPH, *Mechanick Exercises on the Whole Art of Printing*, ed. Herbert Davis and Harry Carter, 2nd edn. (London: Oxford Univ. Press, 1962).

POTTLE, FREDERICK A., *The Literary Career of James Boswell, Esq.* (Oxford: Clarendon Press, 1929).

—— '*The* Life of Johnson: *Art and Authenticity*', in James L. Clifford (ed.), *Twentieth-Century Interpretations of Boswell's* Life of Johnson

(Englewood Cliffs, NJ: Prentice-Hall, 1970), 66–73.

POTTLE, MARION S., ABBOTT, CLAUDE COLLEER, and POTTLE, FREDERICK A., *Catalogue of the Papers of James Boswell at Yale University*, 3 vols. (Edinburgh: Edinburgh Univ. Press and Yale Univ. Press, 1993).

RADER, RALPH W., 'Literary Form in Factual Narrative: The Example of Boswell's *Johnson*', in Philip B. Daghlian (ed.), *Essays in Eighteenth-Century Biography* (Bloomington: Indiana Univ. Press, 1968), 3–42. Reprinted in abridged form in John A. Vance (ed.), *Boswell's 'Life of Johnson': New Questions, New Answers* (Athens: Univ. of Georgia Press, 1985), 25–52.

RADNER, JOHN B., ' "A Very Exact Picture of his Life": Johnson's Role in Writing the *Life of Johnson*', *Age of Johnson*, 7 (1996), 299–342.

SIMPSON, PERCY, *Proof-Reading in the Sixteenth Seventeenth and Eighteenth Centuries* (London: Oxford Univ. Press, 1935).

SISMAN, ADAM, *Boswell's Presumptuous Task* (London: Hamish Hamilton, 2000).

WENDORF, RICHARD, *The Elements of Life: Biography and Portrait-Painting in Stuart and Georgian England* (Oxford: Clarendon Press, 1990).

——— *Sir Joshua Reynolds: The Painter in Society* (Cambridge, Mass.: Harvard Univ. Press, 1996).

WIMSATT, WILLIAM K., 'The Fact Imagined: James Boswell,' in *Hateful Contraries: Studies in Literature and Criticism* (Lexington: Univ. of Kentucky Press, 1965), 165–83.

YUNG, KAI KIN, *Samuel Johnson 1709–1784* (London: Herbert Press, 1984).

INDEX